1 MONTH OF
FREE
READING

at

www.ForgottenBooks.com

By purchasing this book you are eligible for one month membership to ForgottenBooks.com, giving you unlimited access to our entire collection of over 1,000,000 titles via our web site and mobile apps.

To claim your free month visit:

www.forgottenbooks.com/free37818

ISBN 978-0-483-06402-7
PIBN 10037818

This book is a reproduction of an important historical work. Forgotten Books uses
state-of-the-art technology to digitally reconstruct the work, preserving the original format
whilst repairing imperfections present in the aged copy. In rare cases, an imperfection in
the original, such as a blemish or missing page, may be replicated in our edition. We do,
however, repair the vast majority of imperfections successfully; any imperfections that
remain are intentionally left to preserve the state of such historical works.

WARDEN CASSIDY

Michael J.

ON

PRISONS AND CONVICTS

REMARKS

FROM

Observation and Experience Gained During Thirty-seven
Years Continuous Service in the Administration
of the Eastern State Penitentiary,
Pennsylvania.

ADDRESSED TO MEMBERS OF SOCIETIES INTERESTED
IN PRISON MANAGEMENT.

1897.

PHILADELPHIA.
PATTERSON & WHITE.

Copyright, 1897,

by

Michael J. Cassidy.

The Warden.

PREFACE.

THE Eastern State Penitentiary of Pennsylvania, at Philadelphia, has perhaps been the subject of more comment than any penal institution in the United States, or indeed in Europe. It was established in 1829.

The cause is explained by reason of the method of confinement and the discipline of the system of punishment, which was original with that institution. It is the only one so governed in this country, while several prisons in Europe have adopted the plan, more or less modified.

It is unfortunate that misinformation or misconception, and positive ignorance, exists of the methods in practice here, even among otherwise careful and well-informed sociologists.

In addition to this, the many inquiries that are constantly made as to the method of applying punitive treatment in this institution is a sufficient apology, if any be needed, for a brief statement of the principles of the administration and their practical application to the treatment of convicts sent to this institution.

Positive, practical knowledge of the subject in its various phases is regarded as of some value. Theoretic and general observations, however well presented, often fail to impress the inquirers as effectively as the opinions which experience can best furnish.

When the systems of convict punishment, and especially that known as "The Individual Treatment," as applied in the Eastern State Penitentiary, are discussed and explained by competent authority, before those who are expected to be familiar with the questions involved, it necessarily has the merit of authoritative statement subjected to critical examination. It is, therefore, evidence from actual practical knowledge and experience.

When it is seen that the remarks contained in the extracts now presented were addressed to those who were engaged in the administration of systems of convict punishment, and also on different occasions, during several years, it adds to their value, because those to whom they were addressed were competent to understand and criticise them.

It will be observed from the following pages that there are many subjects directly connected with the imprisonment of criminals that are rarely considered. To indicate the range of these subjects and their importance in the study and decision of punitive systems, as well as the characteristics of convicts and their individual relation to crime and the adaptation of punishment to each person, these pages contain information that is of importance because not accessible in theoretic disquisitions, which are often superficial.

It is practical knowledge which long experience makes veritable that will command respect.

The extracts from official reports, and discussions at public meetings of men competent to understand the subjects considered, are here reproduced.

THE WARDEN.

Richard Vaux.

At the Meeting of the National Prison Association, held at Denver, Col., September 14, 1895,

Warden Cassidy presented a steel engraving, and the subjoined sketch of the long and brilliant service of the Hon. Richard Vaux:

IN MEMORIAM.

Hon. Richard Vaux died on the 22d day of March, 1895, from a cold contracted at a meeting with the committee on appropriations of the Senate and House of Representatives of Pennsylvania at the penitentiary.

Mr. Vaux was first appointed an inspector of the institution January 7th, 1842, by the Supreme Court of Pennsylvania, and was re-appointed again and again by the same body until 1873, after which time he was repeatedly appointed by the Governors of the State. The date of his last commission was January 18th, 1895, and was issued by Governor Daniel H. Hastings.

Mr. Vaux was in continuous service as an inspector for fifty-three years, two months and fifteen days, was secretary of the board for nine years, and was its president for over forty-three years. He was president of the board at the time of his death.

It was a high tribute to Mr. Vaux that he was kept continually in service for so long a time, and it was beneficial to the penitentiary. Anyone visiting the institution is easily convinced that as a prison it does not have its equal. Its present condition is due almost entirely to the fact that it has been managed on the same lines for so many years. Its methods have been confirmed by experience, and can safely be relied upon to produce the best possible results.

The life-work of Mr. Vaux is without parallel in penology for it can be truly said that the oversight and care of the Eastern Penitentiary and of its inmates was his distinctive life-work. He was an authority on penology, not only in Pennsylvania, but in Europe. That in which the Eastern State Penitentiary was different at first from any other institution is known in criminology as

5

the Pennsylvania system, and was the outcome of the best thought
of the Quaker element in Philadelphia, headed by Robert Vaux,
the father of Richard Vaux. For many years it was denounced as
cruel and barbarous, tending to melancholia and insanity. Time
has refuted all such assertions, and now the solitary system as
practiced in this institution is commended everywhere, and is being copied and put into practice in Massachusetts and elsewhere in
the United States, and in many cities in Europe.

The separation of prisoners into individual cells in which they
work, as distinguished from the congregate in workshops, is the
peculiar feature of the system. Mr. Vaux was the exponent of the
system, and the Eastern State Penitentiary will never be mentioned
or remembered without associating his name with it. He has
stamped it with his own individuality and characteristics. To
serve continuously for fifty-three years for the good and uplifting
of unfortunate human beings, and that without pay, reward, or advantage, is such a noble self-sacrifice that it should enshrine the
name and memory of Mr. Vaux as a great benefactor of his race.

CONTENTS.

WARDEN CASSIDY

ON

PRISONS AND CONVICTS.

Acknowledging Reception at Chicago, 1884.

At the Opening of the Conference of Officers of Prisons
and Reformatories of the United States, held
at Chicago, December 9–11, 1884,

In response to the welcome of the body to the city by Mayor Carter Harrison, Mr. Cassidy spoke as follows:

I am sure that the gentlemen assembled here from the different sections of the United States will fully agree with me in returning cordial thanks to his honor, Mayor Harrison, for the kind welcome he has given us to his well-governed city of Chicago. From the remarks his honor has made it is evident that he has been no slow student of the question of crime, its causes and its prevention. The gentlemen here represent nearly every State in the Union, and they have had more or less connection with the criminal classes. I may say that the reputation of Chicago abroad is

9

that it is the best police governed city in the United States. The mayor here is said to be the chief of police; and there can be no government so good as a one-man government, when the man has power to enforce his views, and is the right man for the office,— which proves to be the fact in the case of Chicago. No city has more need of good government in this respect than Chicago. Chicago is a large city. Everything is large connected with it. Its hotels are both extensive and magnificent; its streets are large and wide; and the buildings are spacious and high. Everything is big and spread out. It is a great railroad center, and consequently it is a crime-class center. I was going to say that there is no city in the United States which has the same amount of facilities for the centralization, transportation, and distribution of the crime-class throughout the country, as Chicago. New York is a crime-class center. Their facilities for organizing robberies into different sections of the country is perhaps greater than those of Chicago. The police of New York are organized on an entirely different basis. The mayor of New York is not the chief of police,— the government of the force is in the hands of a board of police commissioners. No city in the country has as much actual service performed by its chief magistrate as the city of Chicago.

This meeting of prison officers, as I understand it, is for the purpose of an exchange of views in regard to the treatment of a class of people who make up prison populations, and the treatment of juvenile offenders so as to prevent them from becoming a part of the crime-class. Many of those present will probably take directly opposite views of the subjects discussed and the methods of accomplishing what they desire; but their aims and objects are the same.

I can only say that, from the kind welcome we have received, and the ample facilities that have been afforded us by the proprietors of the hotels and the citizens of Chicago, that all efforts we shall make in the direction of benefiting society will be attributed to the fact, as his honor has just said, that everything great that is to be done in the country now must be done in Chicago. The old order of things has been entirely reversed. Wisdom was sought in the East, and all wisdom was supposed to come from there; but it is not the Star of the East the wise man follows now,—he must go westward, and follow the evening star.

AT THE CONFERENCE OF OFFICERS OF PRISONS AND REFORMA-
TORIES, HELD IN THE CITY OF CHICAGO, DECEMBER
9-11, 1884,

Mr. Cassidy was chosen president, and, on taking the chair, made the following brief address:

Gentlemen and Fellow-Workers in the Same Vineyard: I do not know how to begin; and the important part in all matters that are undertaken in life is in the beginning. But I thank you for this consideration, which is entirely undeserved. If I were to make any apologies for inability or other disqualification, I would simply be following the old routine in such matters. All I can say and ask of you is that you will extend the same indulgence to me that you do to your prisoners who lack the ability to perform all that is required of them. Any errors that I may make will be entirely errors of judgment and inability, and I expect your indulgence in these matters. There is a large amount of work to be done, and I would ask gentlemen to confine themselves, as nearly as possible, to the subjects that come before the conference. Subjects will be submitted covering the whole ground of the management, discipline, and improvement of prisoners, and there will be abundant opportunity for the expression of every form of opinion in relation thereto. Without wasting any more time, let me ask you now to proceed to business.

Organization of Prisons.

AT THE CONFERENCE OF OFFICERS OF PRISONS AND REFORMA-
TORIES, HELD AT CHICAGO, DECEMBER 9-11, 1884,

Mr. Cassidy, being president of the meeting, was, contrary to the usual custom, and by special request of the conference, prevailed upon to open the discussion on the topic of "Organization of Prisons."

His remarks were as follows:

It is unusual for the chair to take part in discussions; but this is the beginning, and all things that are done, if they are done well at all, have to be commenced right. The difficulty in this matter is in the ability of the performer to begin as he ought to. There is no part of the business of prison-keeping as important as the selection of the people who are to do the work. More ability and capacity are required for a prison-keeper than for almost any other business in life. Mechanical trades are taught and acquired by habit. Where individuals are subjected to discipline, it requires a study and capacity that few men possess. There are so many things required that it is difficult to find one now able to cover the whole ground. Adaptability is one of the important essentials of prison officers. There are many men who are qualified for almost any business of life that they adopt; but take them out of that business, and put them into another, and, lacking ability for that calling, they make a failure. Prison-keeping should be made a vocation, not a mere employment, as you would hire an individual to do some work for you. But there are many outside issues entering into the appointment of prison officials, that those who have the appointments to make feel embarrassed in making proper selections.

The guards in a prison are supposed to be nothing more than guards occupying a position somewhat similar to sentries in an army, standing on their posts. Their business is presumed to have very little to do with prison-keeping. It is the general impression that wardens of prisons are generally selected for what ability they possess at the time of their appointment. Frequently, however, their ability does not enter into any of the reasons why they are appointed. Their employés are very often selected for them without any regard to the positions they are required to fill.

One general source of complaint is that politics interferes with the employment of people connected with prisons. That is pernicious, in every sense of the word. While every man in this country ought to take an active interest in the government, the fact of his taking such an active interest, and adhering to the principles of any of the political organizations, should not interfere in any way with the transaction of his business. Because an individual may have preferences, or fixed principles, in regard to government, should be no disqualification for his being an efficient prison officer. But that is not the evil. The evil is that men are assigned to positions in prisons simply because some one of political influence wishes to find a place for them. That practice is wrong. There should be no test of a prison employé other than a test of his honesty and adaptability for the work. It is a fallacy to believe that you can take a man from off the streets and make him a prison-keeper. In all prisons there should be grades of officers. The first grade should be that of the least important service, as far as the treatment of individuals is concerned. The men in that grade should be regarded as on trial, for there is no way to ascertain a man's fitness but by experience in the business he is engaged in. If he is capable of intelligently performing the work to which he is first assigned, he may be taught other parts of the business he will be expected to perform in the future; so that, when a vacancy occurs, you have a man on hand to fill it. The appointment of those people should be entirely in the control of the chief officer of the prison, without any interference by outside authorities. All wardens are held responsible for the care and management of their prisons, and they should not be held responsible for mistakes that arise through the incompetency of persons sent them by politicians or others having influence in the State. The public demands that a warden should be efficient, and that he is the proper authority to run the prison. Where you invest a man with that responsibility, authority must follow. The two cannot be separated. The persistent individuals who seek appointment for their friends are not responsible for any occurrence that may take place in prison. The warden is the responsible party, and he ought to have entire authority over the men who are to do the work. Any mechanic who has been trained to a business requires tools with which to do his work. He ought to be capable of putting his tools in order, provided that the tools are of such a character that they can be kept in order. If he is given a tool that will not bear repairing, or that he cannot put in order, it is impossible for him to do his work as it should be done. It is just so in regard to prison officers. If men are selected who have not the capacity, and cannot be taught to do the work, it is useless to continue with that kind of tools.

I think a training-school for prison officers is very desirable. I would suggest that, at the close of each day, the officers of the prison should be assembled in the warden's office, or some other apartment, and be instructed by the warden as to the manner in which the work ought to be done; the relations they hold toward the prisoners, and the relations they hold toward the authorities. Instruction of that kind will make efficient officers, provided they have the adaptability. The question of pay is a matter of considerable importance. The more efficient, and those longest in the service, should receive the highest compensation. Those in the lower grade, when first employed, should receive the lowest compensation; and as they are promoted, and their capabilities developed, they can be advanced in pay, so as to cover the ground of the smallest salary in the beginning. When it is generally understood that their continuance in service depends on their fidelity and efficiency, and that they cannot be removed except for good cause, they will all take greater interest in their work. When a prison officer arrives at a stage where his salary is, say $900 per annum, he is receiving what would be the interest on a capital of $15,000. He has just that much capital invested in his position. Now, any man who has his capital invested in railroads, real estate, or any other ventures, is continually anxious about its safety. It would be so with the prison officer, if his tenure of office was secure. His great care would be to so perform his duties as to render his position secure, or to keep his capital safe. Until such a system, or something similar to it, is adopted, the prisons of the country will suffer to a more or less extent.

With regard to the inmates,—it requires time and experience, study and thought, and adaptability, to manage them rightly. The training of the prison officers is a very important matter. It requires very little time, and you have all your men at once before you. They are brought face to face; they hear authoritatively what is required of them; there is no conflict of action. One cannot say, "Well, I did not know that; I never heard it before." It secures a uniformity of action, and consequently prevents many errors that are commonly made by prison officers. In the employment of prison officers, the necessary qualifications should be inquired into. Age is an important question; no one should be taken on trial who is over thirty years old. Previous employment should be looked at. All prison officers should be mechanics of some kind. Mechanics are just as easily procured as other men, and their knowledge of the people is better than that of the ordinary men you find in no permanent business. Besides, there are matters about a prison that always require the attention of persons who have a knowledge of mechanics. If you have such persons around you, you can always perform all the work you have to do in a prison without running after outside help. Mechanics who have been brought up to a trade are generally a better class of men. Their temptations to crime and vice have not been so great as those of others who have been living promiscuously and engaged in any business they could find to do.   The best evidence of that is that skilled mechanics do not get into State's prison as a general thing.   When they do, it is generally for crimes against the person.   That is the best evidence that people who are educated to labor do not drift into the criminal class.   Many of them become worthless and dissipated, and will go to the extreme of poverty through dissipation, and then get into the county jail or house of correction as vagrants, and afterward recover and go back to work. They do not go on the road as professional thieves.   There are few persons having a knowledge of mechanics among professional thieves.   There is rarely ever a mechanic among the gang who engage in bank robberies.   It is difficult for them to find a man to do the mechanical part of their work; and the man is generally entitled to the largest share of the booty when it is got.   As a general thing, those gangs have to go outside of their own company for a mechanic.   Mechanics do not make up any part of prison population, and they make the best prison officers when they have sufficient time for training.   The system of political changes should never be applied to prisons in any State.   There are enough other positions, coming under the head of political appointments, to meet the legitimate demand of those seeking such employment; and the prison should be left alone and outside the pale of political preferment.

Prison Discipline.

NATIONAL PRISON ASSOCIATION, HELD AT DETROIT, MICH.,
OCTOBER 20, 1885.

The subject of Prison Discipline being under discussion, Mr. Cassidy was called upon to preside, and upon taking the chair made the following remarks:

I can assure you that however we may differ in methods, in our aims we are one.   The increase of efficiency and the elevation of the character and capacities of prison officers we all have at heart.

Less than two years ago, under the direction of the Prison Association of New York, an informal meeting of prison officers was convened at the Fifth Avenue Hotel in that city.   For the first time many of us met, without any personal knowledge of each other, without any preparation or even an idea of what was expected to be accomplished by the project, nor did the directors of the association know what would be the result of the bringing together of persons of whom they had no knowledge beyond the fact of their connection with prisons throughout the United States.

The conference was continued for several days, and was productive of such good results that another meeting was determined upon, and a general invitation was extended to all officials of prisons and reformatories in the United States to a conference which was held in Chicago, in December, 1884.

The proceedings of both meetings have been published. Much information was imparted as to the management of the different institutions represented, benefiting all who participated in the conference.

All the special interests, industries, and vocations throughout the country are having annual conferences for their mutual interest and benefit, and the advancement of the interests in which they are engaged.

The management of prisons and reformatories, the care of thousands of individuals in the several institutions, is of as much importance to the community as any other public interest. The selection, education, and training of prison officers is as much a public necessity as the training of railroad officials and employés who are advanced through the lower grades of yard men and train hands until they become competent for the higher positions. The safety of the lives and property of the people doing business with railroads, and the interests of the company owning the roads, demand that the employés, from the lowest to the highest, shall be competent and efficient, and to be so they must have a special education to this end.

All the various professions, trades, and vocations in which people are engaged require a special training before efficiency is attained. To take people out of the ordinary walks of life without any special training or adaptation and place them in positions of teachers, directors, custodians, and disciplinarians of individuals under punishment for crime, is as absurd and as injurious to the public interest, as well as that of prisoners, as to commission doctors, lawyers, or mechanics without preliminary special qualifications.

Yet prison officials through all grades are largely—perhaps generally—selected for some personal or political reason wholly irrelevant to the question of qualification.

Prison reform is the principal object of this conference. By that is generally understood the reform of prisoners, the selection of the best system, and surely it ought also to mean reform in the mode of selecting prison officers.

The only way to reform any criminal class is to teach them to appreciate the value of industry. Make labor a duty. Labor is not a punishment in any sense, anywhere, or under any condition of circumstances. One of the usual sentences of the Court, or a part of the sentence, is "imprisonment at hard labor." It was a great mistake on the part of the lawmakers who enacted that labor should be a penalty for crime. The drones of society do nothing, and to make labor a punishment for crime was either a mistake of thoughtlessness or ignorance.

In the institution with which I am connected labor is the essential element in the reform training of the individual, and through it he becomes accustomed to habits of industry, proficient in the use of tools, is made to feel that he has ability within himself for the earning of an honest livelihood; is "coached" and urged—not driven—to develop these, until many go out fair workmen to begin a new and better life, to their own benefit and that of the community.

The severest punishment in our institution is the deprivation of labor. The very first thing we do to an unruly prisoner is to take the tools and material away from him. Labor is a privilege. Many of the prisoners have earned considerable amounts by their labor, and when their work is taken from them, as a punishment, the cost of their daily keep is charged against their surplus earnings. Under the operation of this rule there are few infractions of prison laws, and these few quickly repent and make terms with the authorities to begin work.

But our subject is more directly prison punishments. There is no subject connected with prisons that has been so much talked about as punishments, and scarcely one of which there is so little of actual truth known to the community at large. Since the Prison Association of the United States has been collecting the wardens and officers of the different institutions together, far more information has been developed on this subject than in all the years previous.

NATIONAL PRISON ASSOCIATION, HELD AT DENVER, COL.,
SEPTEMBER 14, 1895.

INDIVIDUAL TREATMENT.

Mr. Cassidy, as president of the Chicago conference, where were discussed at great length, prison construction, discipline, systems, etc., in which he contended for a better understanding of the system administered at Philadelphia, in adjourning the conference, said:

As the time has arrived to adjourn this conference without delay, I would like to express my thanks to you all, collectively and individually, for the great kindness I have received at your hands, and for the indulgent manner in which you have borne with me in discharging the duties of chairman. During our meeting no unkindness of spirit has been evinced, but many friendships have been formed that otherwise would not have taken place. Prison people have the reputation of being hard-hearted, cruel men; but their intercourse with each other here has not proved that to be the fact. I am very much pleased to know that when we go from here there is not a ruffle of unkindness in the breast of any one of us. I extend to you all a cordial invitation to visit the Eastern Penitentiary at Philadelphia, at any time you can make it convenient to do so,—any day of the month, any day of the week, any time, day or night, or Sundays. In conclusion, I would say that, while I like the congregation that is assembled here, I still love them *individually*.

The subject of Prison Discipline being under discussion, Mr. Cassidy spoke as follows:

It would seem to me, from the tone of these papers, that each prison warden made a system of his own, and the whole put together would result in no system at all. Discipline has been confined almost entirely to the prisoner, and it has been go-as-you-please for the officers. The most important part of the management of a prison is with reference to the subordinate officers. Their selection is of the utmost importance. Application is made to the warden of the prison, if he is the authority for the employment of the individuals, in writing. The application must be in the handwriting of the individual making the application, and it must state his age, business, residence, his former occupation, if a mechanic his trade. The applications are put on file, and when a vacancy occurs the warden looks over the applications and sends for the individual and that is the end of the business. He is then employed in the lowest grade of service as night watchman. There may be ten, more or less, according to the size of the prison and the number of inmates. They receive $650 a year. They are on duty from 7 P.M. to 7 A.M., one-half outside in the yard and one-half inside. The half outside pass through the center when the overseers remain all night, so that the safety of the prison is known within at least half an hour. Time tell-tales do not answer the purpose, because if you have those things the officer will attend to his tell-tale if he neglects everything else. Supervision is the proper word. That is the principal guide and the principal safety of prisons. When a vacancy occurs in any of the departments, in the making of shoes or wood work or iron work or anything of that sort, the night watchman you deem most capable for that is placed in that division and he gets $800 a year. When he has been five years in the service he gets $900.

That is about as long as any of them remain, though frequently there are several of that status. In that way you secure intelligence, but they require to be drilled and taught. Prison-keeping is not a business that anyone can pick up, it is a vocation and unless there is an inducement for a man to enter the service and remain in it and improve they are of no use. Every Monday night all the officers of the prison assemble in the warden's office, and then they get whatever instructions it is necessary for them to have in reference to any of the duties that they may be required to perform.

There is then no misunderstanding. They can never say, "I did not know that," or "I was never told that." That method brings the men face to face, and if there has been any misconduct some of them will be shaky and generally it comes out. Misdemeanors in officers cannot be hidden as a general rule. No recommendation or outside influence has any force whatever in the employment of individuals in prison.

Any trivial offense committed in shops would have to be taken charge of immediately, but where they are treated as individuals, and there is no other prisoner to be damaged the treatment may be different. It must be known that a man cannot violate rules without notice being taken of it. It keeps the prison secure from many things that prisoners do in other prisons. Penalties?

There is no law about penalties. You can make no prison rule about penalties. I was surprised at the friend from Kentucky stating his utter abhorrence at giving bread and water. Why, there is divine authority for that. "Thou shalt earn thy bread by the sweat of thy face." The man who does not earn any bread is not entitled to a great deal. Besides it is the most reasonable and sensible way of treating a person. He has time to think over his condition, and he knows the remedy. All he has to do is to send for authority and confess. There are commutation laws and good time laws that take off so much of the original sentence, under the arbitrary authority of the prison warden. They may be of service in a congregate prison, but they are of no practical use in an individual prison. In all my time I know of but one who has been deprived of the commutation law. It is a compromise to assist the prison officers in keeping order in shops, but is of no use for the treatment of a man difficult to manage. Many good men will lose their temper, while others who do not lose their temper get the benefit of the commutation law, and others who are far better do not get it. In shops it is necessary to act peremptorily— to take the prisoner out and inflict what punishment you choose. Sometimes the fault is caused by others round him, and he considers it injustice that they all do not get the same. The discipline of prisoners is summed up in punishment, in training, in means of improvement. So much work or that is the penalty. According to the returns made by prison officers there is no prison system only such as the prison officers choose to invent. The Pennsylvania system *is* a system. It matters not who is in charge the system will go on just the same. The warden does not deserve any credit, because the system is a fact by itself. It will go on all the time.

There has never been any outside interference of politics or politicians or others in the establishment of the corps of managers in the Pennsylvania prisons. We have heard a good deal about politicians. Politics are as necessary as business. Men enter politics for business. So far as honesty is concerned, they will average with the business or manufacturing people of the country. Manufacturers take all sorts of short cuts to cheat one another or other people. The politician takes advantage of his opponent to get ahead of him. Every man ought to be a politician more or less, so long as he does not interfere with his neighbor. Every man ought to stand up and be counted. But politics should never enter into prison management. No one, because he is a member of the Legislature, should have the right to interfere with the staff.

Insanity is one of the bugbears generally advanced by theorists, who know nothing about it, as a danger from the individual system. At one time the Charlestown prison was considered the best managed under the Auburn system, and statistics were kept there for ten years in comparison with the Eastern Penitentiary of insanity developed in prison, and the statistics were largely against Massachusetts. There is nothing in these theories. All intelligent people who have been decent before they come to prison much prefer to be alone. Our cells are large, eight by sixteen, and eleven feet high, and we have been compelled to put two in a room. People come to prison who are not criminals, never were, and never will be. It is not fair to treat them as if they were of the criminal class.

Bank embezzlers, clerks who lived too fast—and that is largely on the increase—bank presidents, cashiers, heads of institutions, all of that sort come to prison, and it is not fair to treat them like the fellow that comes from the slums. They must all keep clean, and those who have tidy habits can do it. They have water in their rooms, and a bath once a week. They have a water closet, electric light and meals served in their rooms without any extra charge. Any one who will take up the subject of the different treatment of people in prison, and will give the Pennsylvania system a fair share of their intelligence will naturally come to the conclusion that it is the only satisfactory treatment of individuals for crime. There are so many new things that come up in prison discipline and in prison science that interfere with somebody else. We get up commutation laws. That is an interference with authority. Now they have got up the indeterminate sentence law. That is a compromise with crime. It is a dangerous procedure in any civilized country to go behind the authority of the properly constituted court, for in the court is the only safety of the citizen. If the determination of the court can be altered promiscuously life is not safe. If there were power to go behind the Supreme Court of the country it would destroy the whole ramification of our government, and the power to go behind the ordinary court has the same effect. The indeterminate sentence and the parole are being introduced in this country in the management of criminals as though they were something new. It is not new. It is not an American patent. The patent right was taken out years ago in Ireland by Sir Walter Crofton and Mr. McConochie. They had all the means they wanted. They did not have to ask for appropriations, but the whole thing wore itself off. The great prison is abandoned entirely, and we take up the idea and launch it out as a brand-new American idea and apply to the patent office for a patent.

Q.—Don't your officers ask you to deal with individual cases?

A.—Always. There is no case that is not reported to the warden. The warden has no private office. His private office is in the center, that he may know what his officers are doing. It is necessary that he should be convenient to his officers, for the first five minutes is the most important time, often.

Q.—How many prisoners have you?

A.—1358.

Q.—How many cells?

A.—780.

Q.—That is nearly two men in a cell?

A.—Yes.

Q.—Do I understand you, that you have abandoned the separate system?

A.—No.

Q.—You have not cells to keep them separate?

A.—No; to our regret. That is not the fault of the system. It is the fault of the State.

Q.—Doesn't that show that the State does not believe in the system?

A.—Not at all. The doubling up of prisoners is pernicious, but it is better to put two together than to put twenty together.

Q.—How many do you have return?

A.—We have the usual number of returns. *What is that?*

Q.—Is there any difference in that between your prison and a congregate prison?

A.—I think not; the best I could ever make out in reclaiming the crime class people is four per cent.

Q.—Don't you consider that it is worth more to reform men, than just to keep them out of mischief? Is that your idea? You simply keep them in a cell without any attempt to reform them?

A.—What do you mean by reform?   Does one individual re-form another?   The word reform has gone into uselessness by the frequency of its application.   I know of no movement of reform that has not been pernicious in the end.   The reformed politician is the worst man possible, often a vagabond and a scoundrel that could not get a standing in the general community.

TESTIMONY BEFORE LEGISLATIVE COMMITTEE MAY 13, 1897.

Q.—How often do the overseers report to you?

A.—Whenever it is necessary; whenever an occurrence takes place.

Q.—Do you have any daily or morning and evening reports?

A.—I have no fixed time for reports.   A prison warden ought to be where he can be got to, at any time, for a report from any of his officers.

Q.—Are you certain that these men report to you all cases that you should know about, as to the prisoners being unruly or in bad condition, mentally or otherwise?

A.—There is no doubt about that, because if one did not re-port a matter the other would, and they would report the delin-quent for not having done it.

Q.—Are these overseers kept constantly upon the same cor-ridor, or are their places of duty changed?

A.—Sometimes I make a change, not very often.   When they get accustomed to their people it is not well to change them.   They understand those to whom they have become accustomed better than others would.   I have made changes; I have changed the whole all around for no other reason than to make a change.   I do not know that any particular result came from it.

Q.—Does it require any special aptitude or qualification in a man to take care of or handle prisoners as they come in day by day?

A.—Undoubtedly it does.   A qualification that we require is that the man must be a mechanic of some sort, that he must have followed a mechanical pursuit or some one of the general trades that are in vogue in the community.

Q.—For what reason do you require that he shall be a me-chanic?

A.—Mechanics are a better class of people than those who are making their living on their wits. They have been brought up to habits of industry, and the others have not.

Q.—Is there ever any trouble between the overseers and the prisoners in consequence of which the overseers are compelled to use force?

A.—Certainly. There is in every prison. I do not pretend to say we do not use force when necessary, and just as much force as is necessary, to accomplish the object, no more.

Q.—To what extent are they to use force?

A.—With any means that may be in their power at the time. There is a club hanging up at the head of the block, if there is any disturbance, and the prisoner makes a fight, he must be subdued. There is no other way to do it. If a man attacks you in the street you have to do the same thing. But no force is used but that which is absolutely necessary, and when the object is accomplished that force ceases. A scalp cut does not hurt anybody. There have been four officers killed in this institution. Three were killed in my time, murdered outright. Yes, there has never been a prisoner killed nor one seriously injured in the whole history of the institution. It would be simply ridiculous to say that a convict prison with twelve hundred people in it, with the different vicious elements that control in that number of people of a certain class, can be controlled by moral suasion alone. There is one element of discipline to be found in every other prison I ever knew or heard tell of, which we do not have here.

Q.—What is that?

A.—Powder. There is not a firearm on this ten-acre lot.

Q.—Then you have no deadly weapons?

A.—We have no deadly weapons. No officer is armed in any way.

Q.—Have you any cells with rings in the floor.

A.—No, sir.

Q.—Is there much trouble at night time, among the prisoners, by their becoming unruly?

A.—No, sir. The general trouble is that they disagree among themselves. There is a good deal of trouble in finding another place to put one. After he disagrees with another we have to put him in some place else. Sometimes they fight and hurt one another before we can get them out and separated, but that don't occur very often.

Where extracts are made under the caption "The Warden's Annual Report" those reports were the yearly official reports of the Warden to the Board of Inspectors of the Eastern State Penitentiary.

Duties of a Prison Warden.

NATIONAL PRISON ASSOCIATION, TORONTO, CANADA,
SEPTEMBER 12, 1887.

Remarks by Mr. Cassidy:

The warden is the executive officer of the administration. The board of directors is the administration. There must be some supervising power behind the warden to control him as well as to invest him with authority. Of what use would a board of directors be if they should delegate all power to the warden?

In the Eastern Penitentiary the warden is elected every six months, and just as often his conduct comes before the board necessarily for special review. That is a part of our system.

No man in any government should be invested with absolute, unanswerable power. He must have some controlling power behind him, or the ordinary human being is likely to go astray or get too large. In his position as executive his authority must be absolute, but there must be a power that controls him. To invest an individual with absolute power, with no one to consult, puts that person in a very precarious position. All individuals are subject to errors of judgment, and I would not wish to be clothed with any such responsibilities.

The most essential thing in prison government is supervision, from the warden down to the latest reception. Whenever that is neglected the whole machinery is in danger. Bolts and bars, high walls and any mechanical appliances that may be invented, will not keep men in prison who are adepts at getting out. There is no stronger or safer prison in the country than the Eastern Penitentiary, so far as its structure is concerned. Men can work their way out of it. Nothing keeps them in but supervision. All employes, no matter how long their service or what engaged in, are better for supervision. Supervision is the most essential thing in a prison. No one is capable of this supervision but the one in authority, who is the warden. This authority is delegated to him by the directors, who in turn supervise him. It is right that they should. No matter how honest or capable he may be, supervision will do him no harm.

All the details of the prison, from the purchase of a box of matches to the largest contracts, should be under the direct supervision of the warden. He should see every individual prisoner under his charge at least once a week, and should be personally familiar with the treatment prisoners receive from their overseers. There is no time when a prisoner desires to see the warden that he ought not to go and see him. He will thus give himself apparently much unnecessary labor, but only by such practice can he make himself entirely familiar with every detail in the institution, which is so necessary that he may justly administer the rules made by the board of directors. All prisons have a ruler. The directors are the governing power. Unless the warden is willing to submit to supervision, how can he expect others to obey him?

Individual Treatment.

FROM WARDEN'S ANNUAL REPORT, 1882.

The opinion generally entertained in regard to the situation of the prisoners in this institution is that they are kept in solitary confinement and not permitted to see any one but their overseer; while, on the contrary, the inmates of this prison have more intercourse with proper persons from the outside world than any other prison in this country.

They are permitted to see and converse with their family, however numerous they may be, once in three months, and oftener, if necessary, and other persons whom the inspectors deem proper to admit; the Grand Jury of Philadelphia County every month; the sheriffs of different counties bringing prisoners visit all the prisoners from their respective counties each time they come; the moral instructor visits the prisoners continuously; they can have the pastor of their own choice, of any church, to visit them at all times; the warden sees and converses with each and every one in the prison at least twice in each month; the overseers are in constant intercourse with them; the overseer in this prison has the entire wants of the prisoner in charge to provide for, instruct in his work, serve his meals, provide the clothing, all of which brings him in constant communication with the prisoners; the school teacher and librarian are constantly teaching the illiterate or serving out and taking in books, which duties make these visits continuous.

ANNUAL REPORT, 1884.

Under remarks concerning National Prison Conference, held in Chicago, December, 1883.

During the discussion of general subjects, when any alteration in the Congregate system was suggested, it was towards Individual treatment; the separation of the young from old offenders, classification, or some distinctive treatment other than the general plan. The more I hear on the subject of the treatment of prisoners, the more fully I am convinced that the individual consideration of each is most likely to accomplish the best results. We are all "individuals," and distinctive in most of the attributes belonging to us.

ANNUAL REPORT, 1887.

From remarks in Report of the Annual Meeting of the Prison Association, held in Toronto, September, 1886.

Many of the supposed theoretical objections that have been attributed to *"the Individual Treatment system"* vanish on investigation of the methods pursued in the administration of it. It strikes the intelligent mind as something valid. It is a known system; no guesswork about it. The individual you have; he is something you can know and investigate. You can form an opinion of him, with some certainty of its being correct. Of a congregation or a mass of people you can know but little, with a view to the treatment of any of them, morally or physically. The more the system of personal treatment for crime and its cause is discussed, it becomes more reasonable and better understood.

FROM WARDEN'S ANNUAL REPORT, 1889.

The individual prisoner, when not surrounded by associates, whose ridicule is more powerful than his better nature, is more susceptible to reformatory influence than in the presence of those who look upon obedience to the demands of authority as cowardly weakness. Consequently, any severe punishment by this method of treatment is unnecessary. There are bad men and men who are dangerous when aroused to anger, in this as there are in all prisons.

Many who have no scruples of conscience, and ever ready to engage in any violation of law, whose whole life has been criminal, and will boast of any outrageous act they may have been engaged in, and have no regard for the life or property of others, may be managed and directed generally by being separated and treated as one man.

Persons confined in prisons convicted of crime have been taken out of society because they failed to comply with the laws established for its government, and are placed in another condition where they must obey the laws and rules laid down to govern them.

The humanitarian sentimentalist and theoretical writers on the subject of criminal treatment would have the whole nature of individuals changed by simply applying their sentimental excuses for the criminal acts that caused the inmates of prisons to be where they are, but have no sympathy for the honest persons wronged by the convict.

Warden Nicholson, of Detroit, Mich., who is one of the ablest managers of criminals engaged in the work, well says in his annual message of this year:

"There is no secret how to properly care for convicts. We have reached that condition of rational development where reason must take the place of effusive exhibitions of sentiment, and practical methods suited to the exigencies of the case supersede the fanciful schemes pushed forward as reform measures. The Gospel unadorned will dictate to an unwarped conscience all that is needful in any case."

NATIONAL PRISON ASSOCIATION, ANNUAL MEETING HELD AT DENVER, COLORADO, SEPTEMBER 14–18, 1895, WARDEN CASSIDY PRESIDING.

Chairman Cassidy said that he felt that he ought to say that he did not agree with any one present on any subject. I come from the old Commonwealth of Pennsylvania. It was the first Commonwealth established on this Continent that came without any entanglements with it. It was a grant from Charles II., to William Penn as personal property. It was never a colonial property subject to the crown. William Penn was a peculiar man, and belonged to a peculiar set of people. His influence has existed up to the present time in the State. The Eastern Penitentiary was founded by Robert Vaux, who was a believer in the faith and views of William Penn, commonly known as Quaker, but better explained as plain Friend. The corner-stone was laid in 1821, and it was opened in 1829. Robert Vaux was the first inspector appointed. Thus the individual treatment was established, and from that day to this it has been carried out. It has been modified, but the idea of the separation of the crime class from others, and the treatment of them as individuals has been continued uninterruptedly, and those who have had the management of it are entirely satisfied, after sixty-seven years of routine work in the same line of thought and management, that it is the only philosophical and common sense treatment of people convicted of crime. There are no two people alike. No two children in the same family are alike, and they are not susceptible to the same treatment. It guarantees that a man shall go out as good as he came in, or it is his own fault. He loses nothing by association. It is not fair for the State to degrade any one if he has committed crime. The punishment of the law is sufficient for personal degradation. There are men who go to prison who, so far as personal honesty and truth are concerned, are as good as any man—persons who have committed crimes against persons. They should not be degraded by shaving the head and eating between a five-point burglar and a black man. It is not fair treatment. There is no prison treatment that will reclaim a man outside of individual treatment. That is the conclusion we have come to after an experience of sixty-seven years. The law that made the government of the Penitentiary in 1829, was that it should be governed by five inspectors, who elected a warden, a doctor and a clerk, subject to good behavior. The law required no interference with the warden in his employment of people, and there never has been any interference up to this time. There was never a shadow of inclination to connect it with politics in any way. We have no objections to politicians. Every man ought to take an interest in politics and stand up and be counted, but it should not interfere with matters like this.

Q.—Then you have two laws that are not applicable to both prisons.

A.—"All discord" is "harmony, when right well understood." Pennsylvania is a peculiar State, and the Friends were a peculiar

people.   They were the first to inaugurate the idea of the ameliora-
tion of the condition of people in prisons.   A society for that purpose was in existence before the Revolutionary War, and is continued to the present time.   I do not agree with all the new theories
advanced by the modern scientist on these penal questions.   They
get so much confused.   It is impracticable to carry out their theories of indeterminate sentences, paroles, etc.   Those were played
out in Ireland long ago.   It is truly an Irish method; liberty under
restraint.   It was exploded long ago.   But there is no State that
has been more interested in its violators of law than Pennsylvania.
There is no reason why a man should not be reclaimed whether he
is a first or a third offender.   While there is life there is hope.
Our system gives every man a chance.   After he has gone through
the fifth or the tenth sentence he goes out and his opportunity for
getting employment if he is industrious, is just the same as any
laboring man in Philadelphia who is looking for work.   He is not
known to convicts.   No one can blackmail him.   It relieves that
difficulty about discharged prisoners.

Q.—Do you use any labor-saving machinery?

A.—That belongs to another question.   There has not been
a word said about labor-saving machinery.   You go and fill your
prisons with the most improved machinery and work against the
laboring man outside.   The free individual is entitled to some consideration.   The State has no right to interfere with him in his
labor, nor to run all sorts of improved machinery against him.
Let the man outside use the machinery, and let the man inside use
his hands.   A man becomes a part of the machine when he works
with it.   The State has no right to make machines out of its
prisoners.

Q.—I understand that under your constitution you have one
prison on the solitary plan, and one where the men are confined in
cells at night, by day work collectively in the shops.   Is there a
separate law for that?

A.—The original law covered both, but the Western people
were impregnated with the idea of making money and making it
fast, and the directors let the warden have his way, and so things
go on as they do in all congregate prisons.

Q.—Then you have two penitentiaries, and one law for one
and no law for the other?

A.—Yes, that is true.

A Delegate.—The only law which causes the difference between the two prisons, is in three words that the inspectors shall have the privilege of assembling the convicts for "labor, learning, and worship."

Q.—Then they have that privilege at Cherry Hill?

A.—No, sir; and they don't want it, and would not ask for it. They would have to get a law for it.

TESTIMONY BEFORE LEGISLATIVE INVESTIGATING COMMITTEE, AT THE PENITENTIARY MAY 13, 1897.

Warden Cassidy being interrogated, in answer to the several questions, said:

Q.—What particular system exists here in the confinement and treatment of prisoners?

A.—The individual system. The aim and object of that system is to have the prisoner treated individually. Each case is studied, its peculiarities noted, and the prisoner treated as his case warrants. We do not propose to treat them all alike. There are no two people alike. If you undertake to treat these people all alike, in a mass, you may as well give every one who comes in here a primer or a copy of Shakespeare's works to read.

Q.—Are there cases here of what is commonly known as solitary confinement, where a prisoner is kept entirely by himself?

A.—No, sir; there never was such a thing here.

Q.—What is the least number you put in a cell?

A.—One. That is not solitary confinement. An occupant of a cell has communication with the people who come to the prison, except the convicts.

Q.—Are you ever compelled to put them in irons, or to place them in dark cells or dungeons?

A.—We have no mechanical appliances for punishment of any sort.

Q.—You have none of any kind?

A.—We have none of any kind; nothing but what you see. We have no dark cells.

Q.—Have you any padded cells in which you put people?

A.—No. Sometimes we remove the furniture from a cell; leave it entirely bare, and leave the man in it. That is one method of punishment.

Q.—Have you any dungeons?

A.—We have neither dungeons nor padded cells. In other prisons they have them to show visitors, but we have none here.

Q.—Do you make any distinction, as to the confinement of a prisoner, when he is reported to you as insane or feigning insanity?

A.—Yes.

Q.—What distinction do you make in the treatment of such prisoners?

A.—Sometimes we take them out all day and have them worked outside, in the yard.

Q.—All day?

A.—All day. Until we determine what it is. It is a difficult matter to determine a case of insanity in a prisoner. I doubt the ability of any one to do so on sight. It requires time, study, and thought about it.

Q.—You regard reformation as one of the purposes of imprisonment, do you?

A.—Yes, the basis of all imprisonment should be reformation of the criminal and protection to society.

Q.—You think, then, that the prisoners here are encouraged to feel that there is something in life left for them, do you?

A.—They are encouraged to feel that they are men; that any one of them is a man as I am, and they are treated that way; that is, we meet them fair and square as men.

Prison Construction.

NATIONAL PRISON ASSOCIATION, ANNUAL MEETING HELD AT
ATLANTA, GA., NOVEMBER, 1886.

Upon the topic of Prison Construction, Mr. Cassidy spoke as follows:

Prison construction, like everything else, to be done well, should be begun at the beginning. You cannot do anything right unless you begin right. Beautiful sites and picturesque landscapes are of no use for a prison. When you look for a site, you must look for the soil first. Get soil that is adapted to take in water and drainage. It requires loose gravel or sandy soil. Clay won't do. When you commence your structure, get ground enough. In a

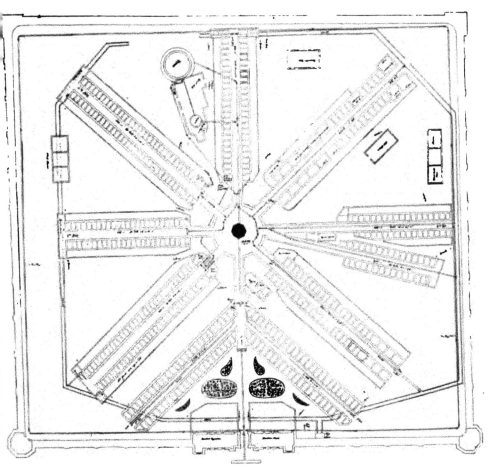

Ground Plan.

more to fear from their own class. We know there is a crime-class, and that it is increasing in numbers. The associations made in prisons do not tend to diminish it.

Work in prison is one of the most important matters connected with the administration of the institution—any kind of work without machinery—labor. Labor is not punishment, although it is denominated as such in the legal sentences. The severest punishment is to deprive prisoners of labor.

The natural soil for a prison should be of a sandy or gravelly bottom, so as to absorb all drainage that occurs. Where you have clay, all the drainage will be held there as in a sponge, and after a time something will have to be done to get that away or relieve it in some way. On a rocky soil, where the water runs over the top of a rock or through a rock, you are not sure to get sufficient drainage from the surface down. The first thing in building a prison is to build the sewerage. Look for a sewer first, and of sufficient size, say three and a half feet at least, with such descent as the nature of the surroundings will permit, you can always have sufficient drainage for the buildings. The size of the prison is not an important question. It should be sufficiently large. The large building does not cost much more in proportion than a small one, and if you have a sufficient amount of room to begin with, you will not be troubled. Now when prisons are built, at the time they are built the ground amounts to nothing in the way of cost, and no building, either mad houses, insane asylums, or prisons, where there are a number of people confined and have to be taken care of, should be more than one story high. There is no reason why it should be more. The cost of gangways and stories would more than counterbalance the cost of the roof for separate buildings. If you have a low roof and any trouble occurs, your men are out of doors at once. The building should be about the size of an ordinary seashore hotel. A cell 16 x 8 x 15 feet makes a very comfortable room; that is about the size of our cells.

Each man works in his cell, but it doesn't follow that the cell should not be that size if he worked in a workshop. I am not speaking particularly in reference to the separate system, or its advantages, but the advantages of prison structure. It is clear that the prison structure of the country is very defective. The use of buckets I do not know anything about, only what I have seen and heard.   I have heard nothing good of it and seen nothing of it.   If a prison is properly constructed, it can be drained just as well as any other building.   For the outer wall, our friend from Missouri says, brick would be as good as stone.   Perhaps it would, if the cost was even, for the factories, but the cell building should be of stone.   A brick is apt to be taken out here and there, and if the wall is of rubble stone, or any good stone, it is not so convenient to make holes.   Sometimes a prisoner will make holes large enough to get into his neighbor's cell.   The furnishing of a cell should be as little as possible.   The best thing I know of for bedding is a buckboard and two light trestles and the common tick of straw that can be turned out and the straw renewed at any time.   I make it a rule to give a prisoner new cell furniture, knife, fork, plate, and spoon, etc.   We furnish every prisoner a new bed, and when the prisoner comes out we destroy the straw, and it can be renewed as often as necessary.   Some people require more attention that way than others.   Water closets in a cell are absolutely necessary, and can be arranged if the building is properly constructed in the beginning,—light, gas, water, and heat.   We heat the cells by steam.   A radiator pipe runs around continuously through the cells, and as much of that water as is not so hot that it cannot be used by the injector is returned to the boiler.   We put it in the pipes with an injector.   You can take the same water back to the boiler if your pressure is equal.   An injector is the handiest method, and is always sure.   For keeping a prison clean, there is no way to do that *only to do it, and to do it all the time.*   There should be no particular time for doing anything; do it when it needs to be done.   Clean it once a day or once a week, but have it clean all the time.   The ventilation of cells, when they are built in this manner, is entirely satisfactory, and you cannot get it in any other way.   There are two windows in the roof, and at the back of the cells; about eight or ten inches from the floor is a pipe about two inches in diameter; that is sufficient to create a current, and as soon as the window is open the bad air goes out.   This is a very important subject, gentlemen, as the old prisons are all defective.   There should not be more than 600 people as a maximum in any one prison.

Under the discussion of the question of construction of prisons and the number to be provided for in each prison, Mr. Wines asked Mr. Cassidy whether it was as easy to know personally 1000 men as it is 600; whether the reformation of the prisoners is the object of the prison, and whether their reformation is a possibility?

In response to these questions Mr. Cassidy said:

There are good reasons why the maximum should be 600. Five hundred ought to be at most what should be in any one prison, but under no conditions should they admit more than 600. Six hundred people of the kind that make up a prison population is quite enough in one place, and is quite as much as one person can attend to, and attend to all the requirements, and wants, and needs, and a great many things that are not needed besides to keep his attention employed all the time. Six hundred is as much as he can look after. Cost should not enter into the question of prison-keeping. The prison should be conducted as economically as possible, but the mere question of cost, a dollar or two here and there at the sacrifice of everything else, should not be taken into account. Some of the men require treatment they could not possibly get where they are massed together, and the warden of a prison should see and know every prisoner he has. If you put 1400 or 1000 prisoners together, it is a little cheaper for light and fuel, and that is about all the difference in cost.

Q.—The difference is still greater in officers?

Not so much, because in most of the prisons of the United States there are no officers; there are *guards*. They are not required to have any intelligence whatever, only to stand guard. The moral character of the prisoners should be cared for, and there is only one way to do it, and that is by one man. The warden ought to be held responsible by the people who put him in the position. There should be nothing between him and his business; we cannot separate responsibility from authority. If you insist on a man being responsible for anything, you must give him authority to attend to it himself; then he cannot say, "My deputy did this," and "This enforces the contract made with Tom Jones," or somebody else, etc. Where a warden is made responsible for the entire administration of the prison, 600 is just as much as he can attend to. Gentlemen, I am a Democrat, but I tell you there is no government that was ever made as good as a one-man government, provided you have got the man.

Prison Construction and Furnishing.

REMARKS MADE UPON THIS SUBJECT AT THE ANNUAL MEETING
OF THE NATIONAL PRISON ASSOCIATION IN FEBRUARY,
1884, BY MR. CASSIDY.

I think it is clear, from what I have heard from the gentlemen from almost every section of the country, that the entire prison structure of the country is defective, some of it terribly bad, and this subject is the most important one that has been selected for prison people, because the structure of the prison is, as the primary school, the beginning. One part of the subject is not stated here on the programme,—the sites where the prisons should be built. The nature and character of the ground is one of the most important things in the consideration of the prison. The beginning is the most important part of anything, gentlemen; if we do not begin right, you always have trouble to go back to some starting-point that is near right; but as long as you begin right, you have no trouble in rearing your structure. Any one that is acquainted at all with the structure of buildings will know that the beginning is the most important part of it, for alterations cause very much inconvenience. My early education was that of a carpenter and builder.

Graded Prison System.

IS IT DESIRABLE? SHOULD CLASSIFICATION DEPEND UPON AGE
OR UPON CRIMINAL RECORD?

Upon this topic, at the annual meeting of the National Prison Association, held in New York, February, 1884, Mr. Cassidy said:

Mr. Chairman: The question now seems to be between grading and herding. Which is the best? It is pretty generally admitted, I think, by all the gentlemen, that the prison structure is very defective; that is the beginning, and I am inclined to think it has been pretty generally accepted that the prison systems of the country are very defective. Hence they are reaching out for something that will take the place of herding. It is proposed to introduce grading. If mankind were possessed of the knowledge of the thought and actions of other individuals, then, possibly, grading might be effective. It is difficult to get individuals of the

Center from which all the Blocks Radiate.

I think not, as a rule. In some cases, association might be proper; but, as a rule, that is exploded in English prisons. They begin with separation, and then destroy all the effects of separation as accomplished by herding them with others. Where you have your own judgment, you can make your selections. Association will work well for a time, but to make it a general rule that every one shall be associated with others for a certain length of time destroys the whole.

Education.

FROM ANNUAL REPORT, 1887.

Education that means teaching by a schoolmaster, with printed books, is very good as far as it goes, but the few hours in school do but little in preparing the individual with knowledge to earn an honest livelihood. The circumstances and surrounding, associations, natural disposition, and family characteristics, are a more lasting education, and are continually at work with their influences, good or bad. Education, in the sense in which it is understood, is at best only secondary as an agent to prevent crime. By a knowledge of reading, such books may be read as will direct the thoughts of the reader in a direction that will tend to form a moral understanding of duties of life. But there is so much written that has wide circulation, with the endorsement of those who are considered authority on moral literature, which if read by weak or viciously disposed minds, will do much to counteract any purely moral teaching they may have had. Many of these books are very entertaining, and generally read by those that do read. The authors are educated, and make use of all the ingenuity they possess to impress the reader of the soundness of their reasonings and sentiments, putting into the individual characters they create and draw their own reasonings, of the line of circumstances in which these characters are supposed to have been educated. Most of these books are but sentimental apologies for crimes of all grades, from the smallest venial offence against morals to the highest crimes known against society. Such books are to be found in most libraries. Victor Hugo's *Les Miserables,* Lord Lytton's *Paul Clifford,* Ainsworth's *Jack Sheppard,* Marryatt's *Pirates,* and Dickens's *Oliver Twist,* are but some of the standards from which the present sentimentalist takes his ideas of crime-life and criminals. Much is said by those conducting congregate prisons of the importance of the hour they devote to night school for the education of their prisoners, but ignore the education of association by which the prisoners are surrounded daily.

FROM WARDEN'S ANNUAL REPORT, 1892.

In this age of progress, as it is termed by many intelligent persons in the community, notwithstanding all the efforts of educational institutions, the criminal class increases more largely in proportion than the increase of population, as shown by the last general census.

There is no doubt that education and learning, being more generally diffused throughout the community, have produced remarkable results in the line of progress; new methods of doing many things have caused many of the old pursuits to be abandoned, and more expeditious and enlightened thought applied in producing results.

One line of industry, or those who followed it but a few years ago, is not heard of any more in the populous sections of the country. The old bank burglar's occupation is gone; more enlightened ways and means have been found that produce better and safer results. There is not now a bank burglar in this Penitentiary, while there are numerous bank wreckers.

The Relation of Intemperance to Crime.

At the annual meeting of the National Prison Association, held in New York, December 20, 1883, Professor Francis Wayland being in the chair, Mr. Cassidy was asked to repeat some statements previously made upon this topic.

His remarks were as follows:

Governor St. John, of Kansas, who is a temperance crusader, had written to all prison wardens, I presume, in the country, to know what influence intemperance had on crime, and myself among the number. He afterwards delivered a lecture in Philadelphia, in which he said that he had done so, and all the prison wardens in the country had expressed the opinion that intemperance was the cause of most of the crime, and the cause of most of the inmates coming to their prisons, except the warden of the Eastern Penitentiary, who said that intemperance was not a cause of crime.

Now, intemperance is not a cause of crime. The crime-class people are not intemperate. As for houses of correction and other institutions where vagrants and misdemeanants are confined, it is largely a cause of their coming into those institutions; but the crime-class proper do not get drunk. Our statistics show that the large majority of that class of people are abstainers. I mean total abstainers.

Then the crime-class, the professional burglar of the higher grade, the forger, the die sinker, the engraver, the embezzler, the people who make their living by their wits and cheating other people, cannot afford to be drunkards, for under the influence of liquor they could not carry on their business. The lower grade of these, perhaps, to some extent are drunkards, but the higher grade of burglars and bank operatives cannot afford to be. They must have a clear head when they are about their work. They can't afford to go with people who take liquor, because they talk too much before or after the act. The forger cannot afford to drink. The bank-note engraver, when he is engraving a note, is sober all the time. The large part of the crime-class people cannot attribute their difficulty to drinking, and do not attempt to do it. They are either moderate drinkers or abstainers. In a barroom, perhaps, where there is a drinking spree going on, some one gets killed. It is not a murder, for there is no intent, perhaps, in the first place for anybody to be killed. Those people would not have been convicted of anything if it had not been for getting on this spree; but the larger portion of people who go to prisons do not attribute it at all to drinking, and it is no more a positive cause of crime than is education. In the criminal—the professional criminal—there is an intent to commit crime not dependent upon liquor one way or the other.

(At this point Mr. Cassidy was subjected to a series of questions, which with the answers were as follows:)

Q.—Do you keep a record of their habits when prisoners come in?

A.—Yes.

Q.—Do your statistics show that men report themselves as total abstainers or moderate drinkers?

LIBRARY.

A.—Mostly abstainers, far more abstainers than intemperate; and from a knowledge of the people we take it as correct. As a general thing, the question is not asked with a view to pry into their habits or to create any prejudice against them for their habits. I would ask a man in this way: "How is it with your habits? Do you go on sprees or take a drink occasionally?" It is quite a common question to ask. They say: "I never was drunk in my life; take a drink once in a while;" or "I don't drink at all." Here and there one will say: "When I do drink I go on a spree." Those are exceptional.

Q.—What per cent. of your inmates are those whose offences are only against property?

A.—About 200 out of 1000 are those whose crimes are against persons, where property has been no part of the offence.

Q.—Then the majority of your men commit offences against property?

A.—Yes, and that is the class to whom I refer as abstainers.

Treatment of Criminals.

FROM WARDEN'S ANNUAL REPORT, 1891.

By the methods of treatment applied to the individual, force is seldom required to secure obedience to authority where but one person is resisting without the encouragement of surrounding lookers-on as sympathizers, as must necessarily be the case where a large number with the same feeling of resistance to any authority, law, or rule are congregated. Persons who have been taken out of the community for violation of the laws governing society for its protection, and placed under a different government, the laws of which must be complied with, will naturally evade and sometimes resist. As they must remain in their present condition for the time fixed for them by the sentence, they must be controlled.

Many of the theorists who write and talk on the subject of the treatment of criminals have had little or no daily intercourse with the crime-class, in or out of prison, but generally conceive a plan or method of treatment that may be very plausible, and, as they think, susceptible of being carried out practically. But when it comes to be applied, it will fail in most cases. With some few inmates of a prison it might succeed, but either general or particular application would fail to produce the results desired; just as architects often make plans of structures and produce elaborate drawings of the same which look complete on paper, but when the practical mechanic is called upon to adapt it and carry its details into execution, finds that it cannot be done without so much alteration that sometimes changes wholly or in part the original conception of the designer.

Just the same results will follow the attempt with one method of treatment applied to persons afflicted with any mental, physical, or criminal disease; for crime is a disease, either inherited or produced by contagion either of environment or association. The best remedy against the spread of any contagious disease is to obliterate the cause. A general treatment for all afflicted with various diseases, produced by different causes, would be as reasonable as to treat all alike for the crime disease. There is special treatment for all other known diseases,—why not for crime? Inherited metal and physical diseases are treated separately, the disease held in check or palliated and sometimes cured, particularly if taken in its incipiency. There is but remote hope for the cure of the chronic crime-class under any method of treatment. Their separation while in prison from others not so afflicted prevents the transmission of the disease. Seaports are protected by quarantine laws and regulations, separation, and isolation insisted upon. Why not in prisons?

To lessen crime in the community, the most effectual method is to eradicate the cause. Parental neglect in the care and training of children is the most prolific cause of contagious crime, more particularly by the mothers when children are of tender age (under ten years), when the mind is new and impressions are easily made by what they see and hear. It is not generally observed how much is lost by this neglect or indifference of mothers.

WARDEN'S ANNUAL REPORT, 1894.

Much has been said and written on the subject of the treatment of persons convicted of crime. Suggestions mostly come from theorists, whose judgment leads them to the alleviation of the criminal, and palliation of the crime committed. Undue severity of sentence or great irregularity in the terms awarded by the courts is often alleged. Where individuals are tried and convicted of crime, and are treated as individuals, equal penalties, or the same punishment for the same crime on all convicted, would not be just to the individuals so sentenced. The law states a maximum and minimum term for all crimes. The judge endeavors to adjust the punishment to the individual, not the crime. The court has the discretion between the maximum and minimum term, and from the surroundings of the case, as far as it is within the power of human judgment, and from the light he has, awards the penalty justly. All that has been done by legislation at the instance of experimentalists in the treatment of individuals for crime fail in results. The commutation law is a compromise with the prisoner, in which he gets all the benefit. The parole, or ticket-of-leave, and indeterminate sentence are for the criminal, who mostly secures the benefit.

Prison Statistics.

ANNUAL MEETING OF THE NATIONAL PRISON CONGRESS, HELD AT DETROIT, MICH., 1885.

Upon the question of Prison Statistics before the Congress for discussion, Mr. Cassidy made the following remarks:

I suppose that the statistics of the Eastern Penitentiary at Philadelphia are more elaborate than those of any other penal institution in this country. Great care has always been taken to have all the details in regard to the prisoner as an individual; the cause of his crime, his environments, his early education, his parentage, all are carefully sought out and put in a table. Each individual is credited with whatever causes may have influenced him to his present condition. That line of statistics has been kept up for twenty years. These statistics are sought after by penologists all over Europe and our own country for information on the subject of crime cause.

The important matter connected with this subject seems to be simply to get the actual number of people who are convicted of crime. It is correct as far as it goes in that direction. But it is also important to know the causes of crime in different localities throughout the country. Disposition, habits of the people in various sections of the country are quite different, and causes which produce crime in some parts of Michigan would not, perhaps, have the same effect in Pennsylvania or New York. It is of as much importance to know why crime is committed, as to know that it is committed without knowing any reason for it. There is no effect without a cause, and there is a cause for every crime. The only way we can prevent crime is to seek out the cause and remove it. Climate and habit have as much to do with causes of crime as many other influences. In some sections of the country the greatest cause is attributed to drink and saloons, and that may be true so far as those sections of the country are concerned. In other sections where there are no saloons, and prohibitory laws are in existence, this cause of crime does not exist; nevertheless there is, perhaps, as much crime in such communities as there is where licenses for the sale of liquors are granted.

It would be an easy matter for every institution having the charge of the crime-class people to keep a line of statistical tables, showing as nearly as possible the crime cause. The reform of the individual after he has become an habitual criminal is a far more difficult matter than it is to prevent him from being such at the beginning or after his first misstep. Heredity is one of the most prolific of all crime causes. The sins of the parents are visited on the child. It is right and proper it should be so. It is divine law, and it is human experience that such is the case. The responsibility is not with the people who have reformatories. There are too many reformatory institutions in the country to-day; more than can do good. There is responsibility somewhere for the cause of all crime. This belongs largely with the parents of children who are cast off and placed in the various kinds of charitable institutions throughout the country.

There is one responsibility for crime, and for a great deal of the crime committed in this country. I have no desire to offend the large number of ladies present, but the truth compels me to say that the mothers are to a large extent responsible for the number of inmates of reformatory institutions. Their injudicious care, kind treatment, apology for every infraction of law and rule of home government, they are responsible for. They frequently apologize for guilty children when the father desires to hold them in check; tell falsehoods to the father to protect the child; stand by them in every wrong until they get entirely beyond parental control, and then shift the responsibility upon some institution that has had nothing to do with the origin of the difficulty. Many minors are arrested on the public streets for infractions of law and taken before a magistrate. The parent or guardian of such minors should also be compelled to answer to the law for dereliction of duty, and upon proof of offense be made to suffer as a partner in the crime committed. If they are thus made to feel practically their responsibility to society for the proper training of their children, they will discharge that duty better, and as a result one large avenue to crime will be closed. The community at large ought not to suffer through increased taxes and depredations for crimes for which parents alone are responsible.

Reform of Prisoners.

FROM ANNUAL REPORT, 1886.

There can be no account that will approach correctness of the number of discharged prisoners that are living honestly by their own industry. Migration is so convenient and the country so large that any figures made on this subject are mere conjecture. Only those who reside or have located in the immediate vicinity of the prison from whence discharged can be accounted for. Letters from distant points by former convicts are not reliable, but are mostly misleading, and in some cases are altogether falsehoods. We know of many in this city who have been inmates of this Penitentiary that are leading honest lives, who are unknown to any of the crime-class, who do not require any police surveillance to keep them honest. They attribute their success to having acquired habits of industry in the Eastern Penitentiary.

WARDEN'S ANNUAL REPORT, 1890.

The strength of the structure will not deter many of the inmates of this and all other prisons; constant supervision is the barrier that desperate and ingenious men cannot overcome. Iron bars, locks, and stone walls are of little use if time and opportunity are permitted. Some kind people think that all the inmates of a prison will remain quietly, because they should be penitent and accept the situation with meekness and humility, and acknowledge the justice of their conviction. Some of the inmates do, but not many. The majority of prisoners do not regret the commission of the crime for which they were convicted; in many cases they use all the powers of reasoning they possess to justify it. Their grievances are against the means that places them in their present position. The law and the administration of it is considered by them to be persecution. Some while in prison profess to be penitent, but few are sincere. The crime-class will generally manage to get all that can be got in, or out of, prison by the easiest methods.

Some of the best talent and ablest statesmen have given their time and money in devising means for reclaiming criminals. Many methods of treatment for people of this class are being tried, and will be continually, for the problem and the successful method for reclaiming the crime-class has yet to be solved.

Notwithstanding all that has been done in this direction, according to the census of the United States just completed, the crime-class has increased much more in the past ten years, in proportion, than the population.

Prison officers are subject to much risk of personal injury from assaults of prisoners, and not infrequently their lives are in peril while in discharge of the duties required of them. The natural disposition of many of the inmates is a disregard of the right of property or the life of any one who stands in the way of accomplishing any unlawful purpose they have in view. The cares and anxieties of a prison officer are little known to the outside community. He must accept quietly his position unless he is sure his life is in peril. He is held to answer for any injury that a prisoner may have received, no matter how violent or outrageous the prisoner acted, attempting even to kill the officer. The prisoners in all cases have the sympathy of the sentimental, humanitarian theorists, who pose before the community for philanthropists.

Religious Instruction.

AT THE ANNUAL CONGRESS OF THE NATIONAL PRISON ASSOCIATION, HELD AT TORONTO, CANADA, SEPTEMBER 10–15, 1887.

The subject of Religious Instruction being under discussion, Mr. Cassidy, having been especially called upon, made the following remarks:

The discussion seems to have dropped into a musical groove.

In the Eastern Penitentiary any prisoner may play on any instrument that suits his fancy, or which he is capable of learning, from a jewsharp to a piano. The time allotted for music is from supper time, or six o'clock, until nine. Some of the attempts made are not very fine music. A few play the violin very well; some learn very rapidly, while others will not or cannot learn at all.

Each prisoner provides his own instrument. There is no music in some people, no matter what the character of the training or their effort at learning. Those who do not choose to learn can listen to others.

Religious instruction in the prison is entirely by personal visitation of prisoners in their cells. There is general service on Sunday morning from nine to ten o'clock, which is the ordinary regular service. The structure of the prison is such that eight different services can be conducted at the same time without interference. The several wings radiate from a common center like the spokes of a wheel from its hub, with a separate door for each corridor. When these are closed each corridor becomes as distinct as though it were a separate building. We have preaching and singing in each wing for an hour. The services are conducted by Protestant clergymen and laymen under the direction of the Prison Chaplain. There is no general Catholic service and no conveniences for any.

We have no chapel. The congregation of the habitual criminals with the first convicts is pernicious. The evil effects of that cannot be remedied by any methods that chaplains can employ. A Catholic priest, assigned by the archbishop for that purpose, visits the prison regularly. More can be done in the way of religious teaching by quietly talking with the prisoner alone in his cell than by the ordinary preaching. There have been three chaplains connected with the institution in its history of sixty years. Chaplains live long in our section of the country, and none resign. They are appointed by the board of inspectors. One visit to each prisoner every month is required of the chaplain. Where specially needed he goes frequently, visiting from cell to cell. He also has charge of the library, which contains from 8000 to 9000 volumes. In the discharge of his duties he cannot be interfered with by any other officer in the institution, but is entirely independent even of the warden. He is appointed by the board, and under no constraint, except in case of misconduct on his part.

There is no other officer connected with any prison who can be of so much service to the administration as the chaplain. In our prison he is relieved from any duties other than those pertaining to his office of a religious teacher. All letters pass through the warden's hands. The moral instructor is relieved from this drudgery, which occupies more time than he can afford to give to it. It is mostly humdrum labor, and another man can do it as well as the chaplain.

We have no schools. A teacher gives instruction to the illiterate prisoners in their cells. They are taught to read, write, and cipher. After that the prisoner is afforded opportunities to develop this primary education at his pleasure. Secular instruction is an important part of prison discipline, but not so important as is believed by most people who are managing prisons.

Superior education is of no advantage to an honest community. Education of the hand is of far more benefit than the education of the brain or the knowledge of books. Habits of industry keep people out of prison; book learning never did. Crimes of education—crimes that are committed and can be committed only by educated persons—contribute a large portion of the criminal population of this country, in and out of prison. There is no part of the community so happy as the working people who earn their day's wages with their hands. The people who make up the population of our prisons do not belong to that class of the community. I think every warden present will agree with me that industry is the best means, in any society, to maintain a standard of virtue. Education is considered by parents in this country as the most essential thing to give to their children. It is a mistake.

One of the chaplains well remarked that the education of the young is neglected by Sunday School teachers and by the church. It does not take charge of them early enough to prevent their getting into prison. That is right so far as it goes. There is no way to do anything like beginning at the beginning. If you want to go to the beginning of children you must go to the parents. If parents will see that their children are properly taken care of early, they will not be apt to get astray. This is particularly true of mothers. They can hold children with a tighter grip than the male parent. After they wander away from a mother's care they may fall into any mischief that comes their way.

The education of prisoners is not as important as one matter that is entirely lost sight of,—that is, the education of the people who are employed to teach them. The education of prison officers is of far more importance than the education of prisoners. Not every man who is taken out of his line of life and society and appointed to a prison office will make an efficient prison officer. I do not care how much book education he has, or how able a man he may be considered by his friends who solicit his appointment. He may, nevertheless, not have a single qualification necessary for a competent prison officer. Prison officers should have a special training to that end. In every prison there should be a school for prison officers, in which they are regularly instructed and drilled in the important parts of their duty, so that its discharge becomes a matter of habit as well as of memory, just as the soldier springs to his place instantly on alarm, from the habit of constant drill, almost before his mind can be brought to act. Such a school should be conducted by one in authority—either the warden or the president of the board of managers. In the Eastern Penitentiary the warden has the appointment of the sub-officers, and he instructs them in their duties. They meet every evening of the week for a few moments at the close of the day's service, and before they go home. There they receive in a body whatever instructions may be necessary for the proper discharge of their duties. In case of a breach of duty, no opportunity is given an officer to say, "I was not told to do that," or "I did not hear that."

This instruction should cover every detail, however small, of their conduct and relations with the prisoners, and also with the public. No act or word, or even thought, is insignificant. No man can go into a prison and take up this work offhand and do it well. Every man within the walls of a prison is different in every way from his neighbor. There are no two people alike; no two children of the same parents are exactly alike. Judicious parents do not treat their children in all respects alike. They recognize differences of moods and temperament, and the same discretion must be exercised by officers towards prisoners.

Much is said and much time and money are expended in the care of children by all communities. Much is done for their welfare and benefit. Education is very well so far as rudiments go, but beyond that time and money are wasted. Industry is the only way to keep people out of mischief.

For two years I kept statistics of prisoners who were news-boys and bootblacks,—a class commonly supposed to be on a plane of life that will inevitably lead into mischief, and they are generally considered vicious boys. It is not so. During that time only three came into our prison who had ever been either a boot-black or newsboy. That is an industry; it is an honest calling; it is a business. They follow that business, they trade with one an-other, buy newspapers and rustle around for their crust of bread, and they get it honestly. When they get too large for this busi-ness they drift into some other calling, usually upwards and gen-erally honest. They have begun by making an honest living by an honest industry, and any change is only in form, and not of habit.

Out of a population of 1055 now in the Eastern Penitentiary, only fourteen were bred to mechanical pursuits. People who are bred to industry do not easily fall into a life of crime. Good mechanics may become dissipated by associations, lose their situa-tions, and get into county jails as vagrants, but they are seldom convicted of the graver crimes, and very rarely become habitual criminals.

Industrial education is the best means of keeping people honest. The labor unions that have been transplanted from the old country to this have well-nigh ruined the industries of America, so far as individual mechanics are concerned. They have almost entirely shut out the American boy from the opportunity to acquire a trade. He is not permitted to enter any establishment where a mechanical industry is taught. Nearly every manufacturing establishment is under some trades union, and the number of apprentices that the employer shall have is fixed, and he can take no more. A crusade against that tyranny will be the best method of reducing the number of criminals.

There are many people who go to prison who are not crime-class people. They do not return. Crime-class people always return to some penal institution sooner or later. Some institutions claim a large percentage of prisoners reformed. I do not like the word reformation. It has been applied to everything that is vicious and pernicious. Yet I do not know any other word that exactly expresses what we mean by it. Crime-class people do not very often reform. The best conclusion at which I have been able to arrive is that about four per cent. of the professional crime-class voluntarily abandon the business. Of first offenders (who are not crime-class people) fully seventy-five per cent. we can never trace into this or any other penal institution. We try to keep minute and correct statistics. They are often misleading, and require great care and attention to get them correct. It is very easy to guess at percentages. It is very difficult with the variety of methods that prevail in this country to get them accurate, and then alone are they of value.

There is no way to reach people for their benefit better than the old Catholic way of the confessional. In that way you reach the individual. Under the system that prevails in our institution, the chaplain, no matter what denomination he belongs to, makes regular personal visitations to the entire population. If anything at all can be done with a man, it can be done in that way.

Motive of Imprisonment.

FROM ANNUAL REPORT, 1881.

To make the institution a paying one has never been the primary object of the individual treatment of the prisoners, believing that efforts devoted to the reformation of the individual, and his moral and intellectual elevation, will benefit society at large more than any pecuniary gains that it is possible to derive from labor in prisons.

Increase of Crime.

FROM WARDEN'S REPORT, 1889.

It is said that crime is increasing at a greater ratio than the population. Such would seem to be the case from the increase of prison populations, but there is yearly an increase of laws to which penalties are connected. Yearly such laws are being enacted by State Legislatures and Congress, which, in some measure, explains the increase in the number of convicts throughout the country.

Indeterminate Sentence.

FROM ANNUAL REPORT, 1888.

Under the head of remarks concerning the last meeting of the National Prison Association, held in Boston, July, 1887:

Most of the experts on theoretical criminal treatment and some of the practical prison officers were caught in the new contagion now prevailing, known as indeterminate sentence and parole, that has been transmitted from England, where it has been tried and failed of accomplishing the results desired. The most successful test of "ticket-of-leave system" in this country is being directed by Z. R. Brockway, who is managing the Elmira Reformatory, in the State of New York, at Elmira. He is doing more with it than has ever been done elsewhere. But he is an exceptional man and has given his life to this subject, and can make anything go that will go.

There is so much plausible theory about the method that is alluring, as are all things that are indefinite. The injustice that must be done in the application of the scheme, the dangerous proceeding of making the decisions of properly constituted courts indefinite, should be well considered in all its features before it is adopted.

The paper read by Superintendent Brockway, chairman of the Committee on Discipline, was prepared by him. It was an indorsement of the indeterminate sentence and parole system, which Superintendent Pillsbury, of New York, did not fully indorse, but signed the report, stating in substance that in his opinion it was not practicable for State prisons. Mr. Pillsbury not being present, and I being the third member of the Committee of Three on Discipline, could not agree to the chairman's report, and gave the following reasons:

I have no doubt you will think it is great presumption in me to dissent from anything that the pioneer of the indeterminate sentence and of the new method of reformation may present. There are many things in this report that I heartily agree with. Much of it is good. But I cannot agree with it all; and there was not sufficient time given to admit of my making suggestions which would not so materially have altered the report that it would have failed to convey what Mr. Brockway intended; therefore I did not sign it.

The indeterminate sentence and the parole I do not approve. I have no doubt you will think me egotistical in setting up my opinion against the prevailing tide now setting in that direction. But life is too short for any one individual to have three or five or ten years taken out of it. Human judgment is the only lever that can be used in determining whether a person's time shall be lengthened or shortened. Human judgment is very fallible. Courts, with juries and with able counsel, are unable to determine the exact amount of guilt or innocence of the person tried. Many times the offense does not warrant the sentence. What Macaulay says is true, that there are several undefined lines that verge so close upon each other that we cannot determine the lines which separate courage from rashness, prudence from cowardice, frugality from prodigality. So there are lines that no jury has ever been able to determine, the line of violence necessary to justify a killing, and the line where mercy to offenders ceases to be mercy, and becomes a pernicious weakness. I would not act as a prison warden where I had to determine the time that a man should serve in prison. Boards of pardon, which are constituted of gentlemen versed in the law, who have facilities for procuring all the evidence in the case, and weighing all the pleas that may be offered, in very many cases err in their judgment in granting pardon, not from want of a disposition to do what is exactly right, but from the fallacy of human judgment. We cannot foresee and determine what is to become of a prisoner after his term expires. "Once a criminal always a criminal" is not true. There are many men serving time in prisons who recover after three, four, and five falls. I would not like to go to the grave with the consciousness that I had deprived any individual of any portion of his life. That part of the report I disagree with, and these are my reasons.

Mr. Brockway has launched a very elegant ship, well-built, secure in every way. (Mr. Brockway, interrupting: "You had better embark.") No doubt he will make a successful voyage; but the most important thing he has entirely left out. He has not provided a master, nor a crew that understands sailing the ship. The most important thing for the people who are interested in the reclamation of prisoners is to provide some means for the training of prison officers, to render them efficient in the discharge of their duty. It is all very well to go over the old ground of discipline for prisoners, and "go-as-you-please" for officers; but it is just as absurd to place an inexperienced man who has had no training at all, to control these men in prison, as it is to place a shoemaker or tailor on board of a government vessel carrying a thousand or fifteen hundred men. Railroads are controlled and managed by people who begin at the beginning. A railroad man begins as a yardman; then he may become a brakeman, and perhaps, after a time, an engineer. But go out into the street, take a man who has never been in a prison before and place him in control. That is not right.

I have no doubt Mr. Brockway will agree with me in some of my notions. (Mr. Brockway, interrupting: "Lots of them.") As I declined to sign this report, I deem it proper to give some explanation for doing so. I hope that you will forgive me for not advocating the prevailing epidemic of indeterminate sentence and parole.

FROM WARDEN'S ANNUAL REPORT, 1889.

The indeterminate sentence and parole is being advocated by theorists and by some practical prison managers. It is not new, but is the Irish system of Captain Maconnba and Sir Walter Crofton, and has been tried in Great Britain, but not with marked success. It is a dangerous experiment to introduce into this country, where the courts have always been considered the safest arbiters of the law. Prison managers and prison officers are certainly not empowered to alter or change decisions of properly constituted courts. The worst people in the prisons get all the benefit of mitigating contrivances, commutation laws, and such like compromises with crime and criminals.

They are ever ready to accept any favors from the community they mean to live off of without producing anything in return. They are constantly a burden on the honest people, whether in or out of prison. On this class all sympathy is wasted.

Prison Dietary, Especially as to the Use of Tobacco by Prisoners.

At the meeting of the National Prison Association, held in New York, February 18, 1884, Mr. Cassidy made these remarks upon the topic under discussion:

The tobacco in the Eastern Penitentiary is under the control of the physician. Those who he thinks ought not to have tobacco he will not allow to have it. They generally all get tobacco who have been in the habit of using it. There is no tobacco furnished as a ration; they furnish their own. If they earn money they can purchase tobacco for chewing and smoking, and can also purchase their matches for lighting their pipes. The matter of injury or benefit to the prisoner is entirely under the control of the physician. If the physician says, "This man is not to have any more tobacco," he does not get any more. It would be a very difficult thing to do to give prisoners rations of tobacco, and make any discrimination between those who should have it and those who should not, because every man will take his tobacco and hand it to his neighbor.

I agree with Mr. Brockway as far as the use of tobacco on people of nervous systems is concerned. Where they are imprisoned, they will use it more profusely than they would if they were out in the world. The great difficulty is to control it in quantity, unless you cut it off altogether. That appears to be a hardship, and is considered by the great bulk of the community a species of inhumanity, to deprive a poor man of the use of tobacco, if he has been using it continually; but I do not think it would injure any one to be cut off from the use of tobacco at any time. I do not think it would produce any physical evil effect. But to insist that you shall not have tobacco used in a prison you make a law, and where you have a law you must have a penalty, because there is no law without a penalty; and there comes in an inducement for people to violate a law. The fewer laws we have the fewer penalties. Sometimes penalties would act very injuriously to some of the people who violate this law. If it is a penalty for a man to bring his tobacco into the prison shop, the penalty would be his removal from whatever business he is doing. It would be a very severe penalty to him for what would be considered by most people a very mild offense. But I agree that the use of tobacco in prison is not any benefit.

Prison Diet.

NATIONAL PRISON ASSOCIATION, HELD AT ATLANTA, GA., NOVEMBER, 1886.

On the discussion of Prison Diet, Mr. Cassidy said:

There is no economy in a short diet. The institution with which I am connected is peculiar. The meals are served in the

GRIST MILL AND BAKE HOUSE.

condition of life or death.   Anything the prisoner ought to have should be and is furnished him by the prison authorities.   We treat all the prisoners alike.   Our cost per diem last month, including all the officers' salaries, and everything, was eighteen and two-thirds cents, of which about nine and a half cents was for food. The friends of the prisoners may bring in any kind of musical instrument from a jew's-harp to a piano, but no delicacies of any kind.   We have two church organs there now.

You know that no man can be a prison warden unless he holds all the lines.   If he lets go of any of them he is liable at any moment to have trouble.   The plan advocated of admitting delicacies is all very well for sentiment, or to please the poor wife or sister who comes to see the prisoner, but we can't supervise those things; and if you let in one thing another one comes in, and it opens the door for mischief that you cannot control.   A prison government, to be a good government, must be a one-man government; and there must be no interference with that one man.   After all is said and done, one man should govern the whole matter. In ninety cases out of a hundred, you will find that instead of thanking the poor wife, or sister, or mother, for what is done for them, they will abuse them because they don't do something else. The convict will ask, "Why don't you subscribe for a newspaper for me?" when the poor woman has just left her washtub or service for the afternoon to see this convict, who has abused her all her life.   No man should be treated unfairly or unjustly; and a man to be a warden of a prison must discriminate between fair, honest treatment and the sentimental pat on the back, "Poor fellow, you oughtn't to have been here."

TESTIMONY BEFORE LEGISLATIVE COMMITTEE MAY 13, 1897.

Q.—Do the prisoners make any complaint about the food?
A.—Sometimes.
Q.—What is the substance of that complaint?
A.—Sometimes a man says that he doesn't get enough.   I make inquiry about it, and in such cases I very often find that the overseer has been in the habit of giving the man double rations, when he has any left.
· Q.—Among which class of inmates do you find the complaints to be more frequent, those who are more intelligent or those less so.

A.—The class of people who have been living promiscuously and getting a bite here and there are the ones who are the most difficult to please in their food. An intelligent man does not, as a rule, make complaint about the food or treatment, or he rarely ever does.

Q.—Is the food the same for the one class as for the other?

A.—The food is the same for all, there is no difference.

Q.—Is any distinction made, in that particular between one man and another?

A.—Not a particle.

Q.—Have you any particular or regular bill of fare for the institution, during the year?

A.—We have the dietary, a copy of which will be found on the table here.

DIETARY OF EASTERN STATE PENITENTIARY.

SUNDAY.—Meat Pie, composed of 1800 pounds of beef, 2 crates of onions, and 20 bushels of potatoes.*

MONDAY.—Soup, composed of 1700 pounds of beef, 4 bushels of potatoes, 2 crates of onions, 8 bushels of turnips, 4 barrels of cabbage, 2 bushels of peas, and 25 pounds of rice. Rice, boiled, 125 pounds.*

TUESDAY.—Bologna, 750 pounds, 1400 shortcakes, 1 barrel of pickles.*

WEDNESDAY.—Soup, same as Monday.*

THURSDAY.—Bean soup, 1700 pounds of beef, and 10 bushels of beans.*

FRIDAY.—Stew, 1700 pounds of beef, 20 bushels of potatoes, 2 crates of onions, 25 bunches of potherbs, and 100 pounds of flour.*

SATURDAY.—Soup, same as Monday.*

Roast beef and potatoes every three and a half weeks.*

Q.—The food detailed in the Dietary is furnished regularly to the inmates of this institution, is it?

A.—It is furnished daily; yes, sir.

Q.—Is it examined, all of it, and found to be in a healthy and pure condition before being served?

* Every morning, fresh bread and coffee, as much as may be desired, the bread being the ration for the day.

* Every evening, tea, as much as may be desired.

A.—It must be right, and if it is not, it is sent back. There is no contract, and if the man who has furnished it says he does not like it being returned, that is enough for us; we have no quibble with him about the quantity or the quality of the purchase we have made. There are no samples or standards to restrict us. We get beef from butchers who fill orders for a large customer trade, and there is a good deal that does not suit that trade. We get the beef off the same cattle from which the customers get it, but we do not get choice pieces.

Q.—What kind of flour do you purchase for the prisoners; is it the best-class of wheat flour?

A.—No, we buy the wheat, and make the flour.

Q.—Do you find that they always make good bread?

A.—Undoubtedly. There is no discount on the bread. Whatever fault you may find with anything else you cannot find any with the bread.

Q.—What is your opinion, in a general way, in reference to the cooking of the food, the soup, etc.

A.—It is all well cooked, and there is plenty of it.

Q.—Have you heard of any complaints from the prisoners in reference to the quality of the food?

A.—Oh, yes. You hear complaints in hotels. If you go to anyone who has been well raised, who has been a gentleman, and has gotten here through some fault, he will not find any fault with the food, only those who get a square meal when they make a stake somewhere, look at it differently.

Physical Care, Liquors, Tobacco, Etc.

NATIONAL PRISON ASSOCIATION, HELD AT TORONTO, CANADA, SEPTEMBER 13, 1887.

Remarks by Mr. Cassidy:

This tobacco question is an endless one. Some use tobacco, —very many use it. Some do not. Its use may affect some people injuriously, just as all people cannot eat the same kind of food on account of some peculiarity of constitution. It would require a revolution and a great deal of expense to eradicate the tobacco habit, or attempt to do it. Tobacco has been a benefit to the human race. There can be no doubt about that. It has created a large industry, both in the agricultural and manufacturing business. It is a source of revenue in most countries of the world. The same might be said of spirituous liquors. To say that crime is produced by liquor is absurd. In the present stage of the world it would be impossible to dispense with alcohol. More than two-thirds of all that is manufactured is used in the arts. Sir Walter Raleigh was, I think, one of the greatest benefactors that ever lived. He introduced the use of tobacco and potatoes. Potatoes have saved and kept in existence an entire nation of people that had no other food and were permitted to have no other.

The use of tobacco in prisons can be controlled; everything allowed in a prison ought to be under control. To undertake to keep it out of prison entirely is to try almost an impossibility. It is unwise to make any rule that cannot be substantially enforced. Every such attempt and failure weakens authority. One of the greatest troubles in English prisons is to keep out tobacco. Prisoners will resort to all sorts of devices in order to obtain it.

We manufacture cigars out of tobacco in the Eastern Penitentiary, and that department is one in which the services of the physician are rarely required. I simply state a fact, and do not attempt to explain the cause.

Q.—Have you not found the eyesight of prisoners bad who work in cells and make cigars?

A.—No, sir. We have had several excuses of that kind to get out, but never a real case.

Prison Labor.

At the Meeting of the National Prison Association held at New York, February, 1884,

Mr. Cassidy made the following remarks upon the subject of Prison Labor:

Mr. Chairman: Labor is the base of prosperity of every State and Government. All that the State takes pride in is the results of its labor. The mistake was made by the devisors of the law when they attached labor as a penalty for crime. It is putting labor in the position of degradation that it is made a penalty for crime, and it makes it odious to people who do not commit crime. The safety of every community is in its laboring population.

Much has been said about prison labor. Prison labor and free labor are precisely one and the same thing; the production of each is the production of labor. The system of applying the labor and the disposition of it by those that have control of it is quite another matter. There would be no opposition to prison labor if it was controlled entirely by the State. There would be no opposition by the outside labor, which we have heard referred to as being in opposition to prison labor and getting the assistance of the politician, or the politician getting the assistance of the labor people to get up an excitement against convict labor. The opposition is not to labor, and not to convict labor. It is to the method in which the convict labor is used, a concentration of labor. The State goes into partnership with an individual, furnishes part of the capital in the way of shops, power, and part of the machinery, and they start a factory together with their interests mutual. It then ceases to be a prison; it ceases to be an institution that is cared for particularly by the State, because the State has divided its interests and called in another party to assist it in doing a work that entirely belongs to the State. The State, by its laws, deprives the individual of his liberty, and by that law he is sentenced to a term of servitude.

Labor is not a punishment. You may make it a penalty, but not a punishment. People who labor day after day all their life do not do it for punishment. The man who carries brick and mortar, which is as hard labor, I suppose, as you can get in the city of New York, on the top of one of these high buildings, when the building is done he seeks some other place to do the same thing. Reasonable, sensible men do not go around seeking punishment year in and year out. There is no punishment in labor.

The State enters into this contract with an individual, and divides its responsibility. The responsibility is what is thrown on a man who has been taken in as partner. The prison official is appointed by the State, subject to the direction of a contractor. He is subject to the direction of a contractor, because the contractor directs the labor and everything that is of interest to the prisoner, and everything in the prison is managed to agree with the direction of the contractor. He must be considered in everything that pertains to the welfare of the prisoner. If the prisoner takes sick the contractor's interest must be considered, and some other prisoner equally as good furnished in his place if he cannot appear in the morning and go to work with the rest. The State has no right to delegate part of this authority to an individual or enter into a partnership in a manufactory. That is where the opposition from free labor comes.

Now much is said against trades unions and the opposition they make to capital, but, gentlemen, there are two sides to that question. Labor is entitled to protection in a government like this, which is governed by the people, as much as capital is entitled to it, and recently the only legislation labor has been able to get is legislation against contract convict labor. The labor thinks that the concentration of a number of people belonging to the State, given into the hands of an individual to operate in mass against their labor, is not the right thing. They object to it. They have a right to object to it. The public account system of prison labor is the only system that the State has any right to employ. It is advanced that the same amount of money cannot be made. If we are to reduce the proceedings of our government like the States of New York, Pennsylvania, or Ohio, down to the vulgar fraction of making a few dollars out of its convicts and selling them to the highest bidder, particularly in a country where slavery doesn't exist at all, there is no economy in it to the State. Everything has to be run in the interest of the contractor where there is a contract convict prison; everything is run in his interest. He makes a contract for a length of time; he secures himself for many years; the State has no redress to withdraw from that contract at any time.

I question the right of a State to bind itself in any partnership with any individual or with any government. It is anti-republican and doesn't belong to our institutions. The great government of the United States will send prisoners from New Orleans to a prison at Albany for the only reason that there is a contractor there that will pay a higher price for them than they will anywhere else; and the management of the Albany prison agrees to pay transportation from New Orleans to Albany and charge the government nothing for their keep, particularly in a country like this, putting their citizens in exile! A man lives in New Orleans with his family and is exiled to Albany. It is not much farther from London to Sydney. It may as well be the same thing. There is no good sense in any congregation of contract convict labor. It is only the individual that is reaping a benefit from it, and he has the advantage of his hand all the time.

No labor is contracted out at the Eastern Penitentiary. The prisoner, on an average, will earn about half his keep. His keep is nineteen cents per day. The average would be about one-half. He earns about ten cents a day. The labor is sold in the open market, and everything made is made without machinery. In all the convict contract prisons there must be machinery to facilitate the manufacture of the goods. The machine does the work, and any kind of people that may happen to come to the prison, either intelligent or not, can soon be learned to move a bundle of shoes from one machine to another, and the machine does the work. The individual actually gets no benefit from his term of imprisonment. On the individual treatment he learns what he does learn. If he learns to make shoes, he can make them anywhere. All the goods that are made are put up on the open market in fair competition with anybody else's goods, and they generally bring a better price over the same goods in the market, from the fact that they are better made than the machine-made. It is difficult to get the kind of labor that will suit all kinds of people in prison.

Q.—The prisoners work in the cells?

A.—Each one in his own room.

Q.—What size?

A.—Eight by sixteen feet.

Q.—Are there more than two to any one cell?

A.—We have sometimes three prisoners in a cell.

Q.—This is in conflict with your system?

A.—It is contrary to our system; it is a necessity. We have more prisoners than we have rooms.

Q.—These prisoners are sentenced to solitary confinement?

A.—They are sentenced to separate confinement and individual treatment, and are not compelled to associate with people that they do not like, or with people that would be obnoxious or injurious to their morals.

Q.—Should you object to more than three in a cell?

A.—I would object to more than one in a cell under most every condition. There may be special conditions where it would be proper and beneficial to the individuals concerned to associate one or two together. One person may be weak, and it requires some one to take care of him; a man may be sick and require a nurse. We have no hospital, no necessity for it; the people are treated in their rooms. If a man is ill, he has a man to take care of him, the same as he would in a hotel if he had the money to pay for it.

The public account system, as it is termed, has always been in operation there. There has never been any other system with the exception of a piece-price plan, which I understand is a new system. We have tried that frequently. Sometimes we can get an opportunity to manufacture goods for so much. We take the materials and make the goods for so much. It will work under some condition of things. Sometimes it don't work so well. We do not make any contract for any length of time. The prison authorities can break off any minute doing any work for any one. It has been some years since we manufactured goods in that way. Since then we have been doing our own work entirely.

Q.—What is the excess of expenditures over receipts in the whole management, including everything?

A.—It would be about $40,000. The State pays the salaries and furnishes the prison, but counties that send their prisoners to the prison pay for the keep of their prisoners, over and above what the prisoner does not earn. All the prisoner earns is credited to the county that he came from. An individual account is kept with each prisoner and his county. Some prisoners make quite a good deal more than their keep. The county gets the benefit of that. The piece-price plan has always been in operation as far as the prison and the prisoner are concerned. He has always worked on the piece-price plan. He makes so much that is allowed for him to make, to cover his cost of keep. All he makes over that is divided equally between him and the county that he comes from. It is placed to his credit on the books of the institution, subject to his order. He can pay it to his family at any time, if they choose to come and see him, or it can remain there until he goes out; or he can furnish himself with some things that are allowed. He is allowed a county newspaper. Each prisoner is allowed to have the paper that is printed in the county that he comes from.

Q.—If he does not earn more than half the expense of keeping him, how can there be any margin to his credit?

A.—You are taking the question collectively, while the treatment is individual. Some individuals do not earn anything; the amount is not divided *pro rata* with the counties. Each individual pays his county just what he earns. Some men will earn from $1.50 to $2.00 a day on some kinds of work,—experts. Another man will not earn anything,—an incapable, a cripple, a lunatic.

Q.—Have you any arrangement by which you provide employment for the prisoner after he leaves you?

A.—None, sir. It is supposed that he is not known in the community, and his opportunity for getting employment is just as good as any other man's that is seeking employment in the street. He is not known in the criminal class unless he was acquainted with them before he came into prison. When he gets out, his opportunity for employment is just as good as any other man's in the community.

Q.—Have you means of saying what percentage you receive back of those who leave you?

A.—Our reports give us all the minute details of reconvictions and every other kind of data. I do not carry the figures always with me. We keep a very correct account of all statistics that possibly can be gathered, and our reconvictions are much more than they ought to be.

Q.—Mr. Round stated they were 65 per cent. in that (N. Y.) State. Do you suppose they are as high as that in Pennsylvania?

A.—The reconvictions to our prison would not run over 25 per cent.; that is, of persons discharged from our prison; but reconvictions would run up as high as 50 per cent. for men who had been in other prisons. There is no intelligent way of treating people, only individually. It may be the most expensive, on the surface, to the State, but it is the least expensive in the long run, with better results both to the individual prisoners and to the community that they belong in, and better results to the prison officials. They are more easily managed, less reason for any punishment of any kind. We have no necessity for any punishment in the individual's treatment, no reason for it.

Q.—It used to be largely charged upon your system that it promoted lunacy?

A.—That has been alleged. There has been no foundation in fact for it. There has always been a persistent opposition to the individual system in this country. The opposition and the sides taken on the subject assume the violence of political partisanship without any regard to reasoning out the question; but I am very glad to know that all the changes that are proposed by the gentlemen who have been managing the congregate system, all tend towards individualization. First, you propose to abandon herding together, and go to grading. That is one long step. Do you propose to get away from congregation, and go to classification? Now, you have only to go one step further—and it is not a long one—separation, individualization. It is the only reasonable, philosophical method of treating people. There are no two people made alike, no two people constituted in their physique, in their disposition, or in their habits alike, and they cannot be treated alike and treated properly. The men who come to prison who are guilty of no crime are few. There are some. There are many who come to prison who are guilty of crimes against persons where property has been no part of the offense—not murders; they are convicted for murder, but they were really killings, manslaughters, violent assault and batteries. As far as truth and honesty is concerned, those men are as good as any man in the community in which they live. Why should they be compelled to associate with people who will damage them for life by reason of their knowledge of them, that would meet them wherever they could?

I wish to reply to what Professor Wayland said of the trades learned in prison, and the amount that the prisoner can earn while learning a trade. Boys, years ago, had to serve five years to learn any trade; people who come to prison cannot earn wages at mechanical work immediately. Trades are not got ready-made. It takes time and money expended in loss of material while they are learning this trade. We teach all our people trades that we can.

Prison Labor, and Answers to Miscellaneous Questions in Reference to the Separate System.

AT THE CONFERENCE OF OFFICERS OF PRISONS AND REFORMA-
TORIES, HELD AT CHICAGO, DECEMBER 9-11, 1884,

by unanimous request of the members, the chairman, Mr. Cassidy, made the following remarks upon

PRISON LABOR.

The laborer is worthy of his hire. The question of labor throughout the country has been pretty generally discussed during the last four or five months, and the rights and wrongs of labor have been pretty fully ventilated. The capitalists and the people who are employed to do the labor do not agree upon the terms, and there is a constant irritation throughout the country on this subject. While capital has had all the legislation to protect itself that it has ever asked for or required, the other side has had very little legislation. The only legislation that the laborers have succeeded in getting on this subject has been in regard to contract prison labor. The State takes charge of an individual for the commission of crime; no other authority has any right to take charge of him. That authority is vested in the State. The prison officers of a State are the recognized authorities for the care of the people whom the State has taken charge of, and relieve them of the responsibility of taking care of themselves. When the State assumes that charge of an individual, no statute law of any State gives it power to delegate that authority to other but the legalized officers of the State.

The great States, like Illinois, New York, or Pennsylvania, should not traffic in the labor of the people whom they have taken by compulsion from the walks of labor, and hand it over to people who farm it out as a business. That is not becoming in a great commonwealth. The laboring people of the country have some rights that ought to be respected, and there are two sides to this question, look at it as we may. An individual furnishes a certain amount of capital; the State furnishes an equal amount of capital,— if not in money, in property; there is a partnership entered into between the State and an individual to run a factory of some kind, to carry on a manufacturing business together, and the profits are not equally divided. It is asserted that the State receives more profit from a system of contract labor than it would by carrying on business for itself. It is asserted by people who have charge of prisoners that, under the contract system, they have been able to get more remuneration for the labor of their prisoners; why that should be so has never been clearly explained by any of them. The only explanation that has been made,—and it is an unsatisfactory and very humiliating one to make,—is that it is owing to the lack of capacity of the people who have charge of the prison. One individual contractor will take hold of the labor of a prison and manage his business at a profit. All the business that is done is done by this individual contractor. What else is required to be done in a prison, so far as thought and labor are concerned, does not amount to much. If a prison warden has not the capacity to manage his prison and manage its labor, why should not the State give the contractor the miserable salary it pays its warden, and let him be warden and contractor too? They assert that an individual cannot do this. An individual does do this, all but looking after the clothing of the prisoners and furnishing them with their food, and that is done by contract; the prison officers have little to do with the matter. I do not say that the prison officers have very little to do; they are poorly paid for what they do do. They cannot do anything else; they are unfitted for other business. After being associated for a term of years with the worst classes of the community, it is natural to suppose they would be unfitted for any other business outside of that.

In favor of the contract system, it is asserted that prisons have been running in debt under the State authority. The causes of this running in debt have not been given. It is not the change of system and the manner of doing the work that makes the difference. In New York and other prisons, where the State account has been a failure, it was the stealing. The money sunk by the State of New York in this work was stolen by the people who had the management of it. It does not follow that the system of State account was responsible for the loss in their business; but they will make a comparison between the loss then and the increase now. Manufacturing business, at the time the State account was in operation, was dull, and there was little remuneration for it, just as it is now, when we are running on a very shallow bar in the way of business all over the country. It is no part of the business of prison wardens, however, to say what the State shall determine in regard to the employment of its convicts; their only business is to care for them in the best manner they know how. Any expression on the subject of convict labor would come with a bad grace from the people who are managing prisons; that is a matter entirely for legislation. Our business is confined strictly to the administration of the prison, and I hope that we will not put ourselves in the ridiculous position of committing any number of prison wardens to a subject that is of no use to discuss. Every warden present may say, with both hands up, that he cannot manage his prison without contract labor. It matters not what we say; the declaration has gone forth, and the people will not sustain convict contract labor. The noisy people have condemned the system, and the demagogue, and any one who can make any capital

Room in Eighth Block.—Knitting Hosiery.

in. Where you have a single individual to treat you can treat him just as his case deserves. When you have a shop full of people, and you have to treat one individual in that shop, you have to treat him so that you will not offend the rest and demoralize them. Therefore, you cannot treat him properly; you cannot treat him as his case requires. In the first place, the contractor does not want him treated. He does not want the man to lay idle three or four days, until he will resume work cheerfully. I have never had actual experience, but that is where the experience, I think, will come in.

Q.—Those who have had experience do not find it so.

A.—Well, I am free to say that it is easier to run a prison with somebody else to do it than to do it yourself. But this subject of labor is a very serious one both in and out of prison, and it is a thing that requires the adjustment of legislation. No legislation, probably, can improve the condition of both parties. Nothing can affect that but the natural law of supply and demand. All legislation which attempts that is futile, because it never has, and never can, operate. There is a law of supply and demand which controls the market. It is belittling to a great commonwealth like Illinois, which covers more territory than the kingdom of England, to be hesitating about a question of how much money can be made out of the convict class. The State should take the entire charge of convicts within its borders. It should furnish them with labor, dispose of the goods, and regulate everything in regard to the prisons. Perhaps that would do some men injustice who have money invested in prison contracts; but I understand many of them would be glad to throw up their contracts, not because there is not a prospect of having them renewed in the future, but because there is a depression in business, and they cannot sell their goods. I have no doubt they would like to be relieved of the contracts they have made to supply the convicts with labor.

Q.—What is the amount of your appropriation?

A.—Forty thousand dollars, which pays the expenses, keeps the building in repair, and carries on the library.

Q.—Does it feed the prisoners?

A.—No, the support and maintenance is paid by the county sending the prisoners. All the prisoners earn is credited to the county. If there is any deficiency the county pays the difference at the end of the year. Some prisoners earn a great deal more than their keep, and return a profit to the county.

Q.—Does a prisoner get any portion of his earnings if he makes more than his support?

A.—He gets one-half of what he earns above his keep.

Q.—What is the average cost to the county?

A.—Last year it was nineteen and a half cents per diem per capita.

Q.—In addition to the earnings?

A.—No; that was the actual cost of the keep per diem per capita. That includes everything except salaries, repairs, libraries, etc.

Q.—Everything over the $40,000.

A.—Yes; that is the actual cost. What a prisoner earns above that the county gets credit for half, and he gets credit for the other half.

Q.—What is the average number of your inmates?

A.—A little below 1000. The whole population would be about 1600.

The prisons that are self-sustaining, under the contract system, do not give us all the figures pertaining to the work. In New York they have a number of prisons, and they only give us figures for Sing Sing, which shows very large earnings, much to the credit of Warden Brush. They rarely tell us that Clinton costs from $50,000 to $75,000 a year, and that Auburn loses money, or mention the thousand prisoners on Blackwell's Island from which there is no return.

Q.—They are not State prisoners?

A.—No, but they are in the State, and earn nothing. In Clinton they lose a great deal of money, and they never tell us that. The great State of Pennsylvania ought to take credit for being able to pay for taking care of its convicts, and giving them an opportunity of doing right when they leave prison. No criminal forms bad associations there. He goes out just as good as he goes in, and his chances of earning bread when he is discharged are just as good as any of the fifty thousand persons in Philadelphia who have to go out day by day and ask for work.

Q.—Don't you think his treatment has improved his chances for securing work?

A.—Yes, his chances are very much improved, because he has been educated to do something.

Q.—Have you any statistics from which you can found an

estimate of the percentage of reconvictions of the men you discharge?

A.—The reconvictions of the crime-class of people to our
prisons are the same as to other prisons.

Q.—What is the percentage?

A.—The reconvictions of habitual convicts to our institution
alone are about 25 per cent. Our total reconvicts from all penal
institutions form about 50 per cent. of the prison population.

Q.—What do you call the crime-class?

A.—Professional thieves.

Q.—Then your system does not reform any more than any
other system?

A.—Not of that class of people. Seventy-five per cent. of
those who are convicted for the first offense are never heard of at
all.

Q.—Then wherein is your prison better than any other in
regard to the percentage of men reconvicted?

A.—The young man who goes into a prison on the congregate plan is thrown among the worst class of people, and he is
ridiculed out of all good intentions he may have. There is nothing that will cause a young man to go over the line of rectitude
quicker than ridicule.

Q.—That is theory; but do other prisons show a larger percentage of returns?

A.—Yes, they do.

Q.—Do the statistics show that fact?

A.—I think they do.

We know that under the individual treatment they do not
form bad associations. Whatever that advantage may be, we have
it. We are inclined to think that it is an advantage. Our system
is carried on by the authority and under the laws of the State.
The Pennsylvania system is known all over the world. It origi-
nated in the Eastern Penitentiary. The first prison was organized
in Allegheny on the separate plan. The Eastern Penitentiary was
commenced in 1821, and was first occupied in 1829, and has been
in successful operation for fifty-five years. It has consequently
gone far beyond any experiment. It has been adopted in the
principal states of Europe. The best prisons in Europe to-day are
those conducted on the separate system. The best prisons of
France and Italy are modeled on the Pennsylvania plan. While

we may disagree in regard to the employment of the people, the Eastern Penitentiary has been managed admirably on the convict contract labor system. There is no better managed prison in this country. Our system is a little more expensive, but it is claimed that it is more beneficial to the community; and what conduces to the best interests and protection of society is the best thing for the State to adopt.

Q.—How do they work in your prison?

A.—Each individual works in the cell he occupies at shoe-making, tailoring, shirt making, cigar making, stocking making, etc. The cells are rooms with no appearance of prison cells about them. They are eight by sixteen feet, and twelve feet high. They are furnished with a water-closet, water and gas, means of bathing, and meals are served in the rooms without extra charge.

The prisoners are compelled to do their own laundry work, that is so far as their own clothes are concerned. They are allowed to have their own under-clothes, providing they take care of them themselves.

Q.—How do you instruct them in their work?

A.—The officers do the instructing. In a block where shoe-making is carried on, all the officers are practical shoemakers. They give each man his work and instruct him how to do it, see that it is properly done, and return it to the superintendent who has charge of the department. All the prisoner requires is furnished by the officer, and what he is entitled to have is supplied him immediately.

Q.—Does the prisoner ever step outside of his room?

A.—There is a yard attached to each room on the ground floor, where he is let out to exercise every day.

Q.—The yard is simply a cell without a roof to it?

A.—Yes; a ten-acre lot would, under the circumstances, be a cell without a roof to it.

Q.—How many cells have you?

A.—Seven hundred and thirty.

Q.—And how many prisoners?

A.—One thousand and fifty-six.

Q.—Then the solitary system is not fully carried out?

A.—No, not fully, on account of lack of rooms.

Q.—How near together are the cell yards? Could a prisoner throw a note over the walls?

A.—Certainly; you can throw a note over a fence forty or fifty feet away. It is all nonsense to think you can make a prison that cannot be overcome by the people occupying it. Supervision is the only thing that can keep prisoners in order. Fences can be scaled, and the locks on banks do not prevent people breaking in; it is the supervision that does it, and we claim to have careful supervision in the prison. There are men who can get out of any prison if they have the opportunity; and there is nothing that can be put up by any man that some other man cannot put down. What keeps convicts in check is supervision.

Q.—How are the Sunday exercises conducted?

A.—By the doors of the cells being opened. The prisoners do not see each other. We have ten corridors and ten preachers going at once, and if salvation cannot be reached by means of ten preachers, it cannot be reached at all.

Q.—Do you consider preaching a means of discipline in your prison?

A.—It is not an infliction.

Q.—Are the preachers under pay?

A.—No, sir; they are not under pay. One has charge of the library and all the educational matters attached to it. There is no other prison in the world like ours, and gentlemen who have not seen it do not understand it. Each cell building is separate. There is no loft or pigeon-holes to put fellows in. There are 100 cells in one corridor, and 136 in another that may be alongside of it. The building is octagon, and the cell buildings radiate from it. Anything occurring in one building will not be seen or heard in another. Four of the corridors are two stories high, which is a mistake. There is no reason why they should go higher. We are free from the danger of epidemics, each man being treated in his own cell. There are peculiarities about the instruction, management, and detail of a separate prison that cannot be properly explained on an occasion of this kind.

I would like to have every one here, should he ever pass through Philadelphia, visit and inspect the Eastern Penitentiary. I think the separate system is the only philosophical method of treating people. People are not made alike, and they cannot be treated alike. I might as well take an educated man and give him a spelling book, and tell him that was fit reading matter for him, or take an illiterate man and give him Shakespeare, and tell him that is the kind of literature he should have. Individual tastes and habits have to be looked into in reformatory as well as in other work.

Q.—Does not solitary confinement affect the health of prisoners?

A.—They go out enjoying better health than when they came in.

Q.—But how in regard to those who do not go out?

A.—Those who do not go out have better health. I may state further, in answer to this question, that our prisoners do not "go" out,—they are "let" out when their time expires.

Q.—What is your death-rate?

A.—Our death-rate this year has been about sixteen in 1600.

Q.—Are your men pardoned out to prevent them from dying in prison?

A.—No, sir; there have been cases of that kind, but very rarely. It has been held that the sickness of a prisoner is no condition for his pardon.

Q.—What is your insanity-rate?

A.—About the same average as other prisons. I have fifty insane people now.

Q.—Several years ago there was a comparison made of the percentage of insanity in the Massachusetts prison and in yours, and the report was against the Massachusetts prison?

A.—Yes, sir; that is correct. There is no ground for the charge that the separate system produces insanity; that idea was exploded long ago. No one is removed from our prison because he is insane. Of the fifty insane persons now there, five have developed insanity since their admission; the other forty-five were tainted long before they came. They are the source of a great deal of trouble, but I am not prepared to say that I am not able to take care of insane people as well as any others, and I must say that before I can get them removed many of them are safer with me and less dangerous to their associates than they would be in any insane asylum. The overseers are responsible people. They have been subjected to a training that renders them equal to any business connected with the institution. After they have served five years they receive a salary of $900, which is equivalent to a capital of $15,000 invested at six per cent. They have great care for that capital, and are anxious to retain their situations; and the only way to retain them is by fidelity to the service. They are fully aware of that, and at no time is there any danger of a break-down in consequence of a warden dying or a keeper getting killed. The work will go along just the same. When I am away I leave the prison in charge of a chief officer, whom I designate, and all orders are obeyed just as if I were there myself. We have thirty-two officers altogether.

Q.—You have no free men employed?

A.—No, sir; no one is engaged in the prison in any way, or in any capacity, other than those employed by the State. There has never been a contract made for anything since the corner-stone was laid.

Q.—Do you have many armed guards?

A.—The night watchmen who patrol the wards have revolvers. There are no other firearms on the ground, and no officer is allowed to carry them. There is no necessity for force under our system. The instructors in labor go into the cells alone and instruct the prisoners.

Q.—How many persons does the prisoner see?

A.—He sees the officers, the moral instructor, and the warden at least every two weeks. The law is that the warden shall see every prisoner in his charge every day, but that could not be; I see them every two weeks. The acting committee for the Society for the Alleviation of the Miseries of Public Prisoners come in every once in a while to see the prisoners.

Q.—Have you a uniform?

A.—We have no uniform. We make the goods we use in our own looms. We are not particular about the color.

Q.—How do you get dinner into the cells?

A.—Just the same as a waiter would hand it in at the door of a room in a hotel. The food is prepared by convict labor; we employ no one outside the prison. There are many peculiarities about this system that I cannot explain unless I am questioned a great deal. So far as its being a success in the treatment of individuals is concerned, that is beyond question; there is no doubt about that now. Writers, however, will refer to the old prejudices against it. De Tocqueville wrote about it. When Dickens came to this country he visited the prison, and on his return he wrote very damaging things about it, as he did about everything relating to this country which he described. He wrote a pathetic story about a Dutchman who had been sentenced for five years, and who had asked him, with tears in his eyes, if he could live the sentence out. That was forty-two years ago, and yet it was only last year that Charles Langheimer, Dickens's Dutchman, died; and he had been fourteen times in the prison since Dickens saw him, and did not die but once,—and that was the last time. He died in prison. He came there the last time a sick, broken-down old man. He would not go to the workhouse, and asked me to take him in. I took him in, and he remained until he died.

Q.—Do you give your prisoners any holidays?

A.—Our prisoners have holidays, but no excursions. They generally work on the regular holidays, and do more work than they do on other days, and on those days they are not charged for their keep. Last year very little short of $10,000 was paid to the families of prisoners as their share of the earnings. A man's wife comes to see him, as a rule, once in three months. She may have two or three children and no means of supporting them except by what she can earn. She gets five or six dollars when she comes to see her husband; and if work is plenty, she comes before the time is out, and may get three or four dollars, which is a great deal to a person who has nothing. That, at any rate, would be the sentimental view of it. This plan, however, enables the prisoner to keep his family together, and have a place to go to when he is discharged.

Q.—Have your prisoners absolute control of that money?

A.—No, sir; but they can give it to their families. They can purchase certain things which they are allowed to have with it. We allow them tobacco and pipes, but not cigars. They subscribe for the papers of their counties and the literary papers. It would not do to admit all the papers of the country, for it would create a good deal of confusion, cause an amount of work, and do no possible good. Some papers are selected that they are allowed to subscribe for, such as the New York *Herald*, Philadelphia *Weekly Press*, and *Weekly Times*.

Q.—Do you clip the papers before giving them to the prisoners?

A.—No, sir; that would be useless, because they would get the news from their county papers, and it is a matter of no great consequence.

Q.—Do you supervise their correspondence?

A.—Yes, sir; the correspondence is supervised throughout. They write once in four weeks, and are allowed to receive all proper letters that come for them.

Prison Labor.

FROM ANNUAL REPORT, 1888.

In some instances, labor is awarded as part of the penalty; hard labor, as the sentence in many cases reads, was, by the jurists who framed the laws, no doubt intended as a punishment to the individual so sentenced for the crime he had been convicted of. Labor may be a penalty, and it is the part of the sentence which is most cheerfully complied with, and paid without grumbling, and is in no sense regarded by inmates of prisons as a punishment.

Labor performed by honest persons in the community is considered a duty. The maintenance of families and most of the pleasures and enjoyments of life depend on labor and its products.

Industry is the surest prevention of crime. To teach habits of industry, promote education of labor, debar idleness in the habits of young first offenders, will do much toward preventing them falling into the crime-class.

Hand-made articles, shaped and fashioned with hand tools, without the aid of power machinery, is the most intelligent method of employing prisoners for their future benefit, besides giving them that physical exertion necessary to their condition of health.

The amount of production of articles made in all the prisons of the United States by prisoners alone, without the aid of machines and contractors, and their numerous employés who are not connected with the prison in any official capacity, would have no more visible effect on the general industries of the country than a shower of rain would have on the volume of water in Lake Michigan.

Prison Labor.

FROM ANNUAL REPORT, 1881.

We teach trades not as a punishment but as an incentive to reform, and to give the idea to the prisoner that an honest life is best secured by industry. That is my view of labor, in prisons and everywhere.

Most of those who have come to prison claiming to have a knowledge of some handicraft or trade are those who have spent but a few months, or at most but a year or two, at their business, but have never pursued it as a settled means of living.

Among rewards for good conduct are a reduction of term of sentence, and the privilege of making overwork.

The money thus made is paid to the prisoner on his discharge, or to his family during his imprisonment, or it may be expended in such articles as the rules of the institution will admit, excluding everything in the nature of provisions; the law of the State being that no prisoner shall receive anything but the prison allowance, which has always been rigidly adhered to.

But, at the same time, good conduct and industrious habits are not always a reliable indication of the moral status of a prisoner; for, as a general rule, we find that "professional" men, as they are termed, are among the best behaved and not unfrequently the most industrious, not from an honest love of industry, but because constant employment is found to be the best means to obey rules and for preserving their health.

In the maintenance of good order and discipline, and, indeed, in everything that pertains to the well-being of the prisoners, much depends upon the overseers, and it gives me pleasure to acknowledge the uniform disposition evinced by those connected with the institution to do all in their power to promote these most desirable objects.

From Annual Report, 1887.

Industrial mechanical training, without the aid of any artificial power other than the physical force of the individual, educates both the mental and physical faculties, keeping the mind constantly active in guiding the hand that fashions the articles being produced. By this constant occupation the time appears to pass more rapidly, giving the worker that cheerful feeling of contentment that remunerative labor produces. When the worker has a share of the production of his head and hands, he feels an independence and a self-sustaining power within himself that enables him to contemplate his future without fear of being dependent on charity or to the violation of law in order to subsist. Many of the discharged prisoners have money due them from overwork, which enables them to present a respectable appearance, and greatly facilitates them in getting employment in the line of their knowledge of work acquired while in this institution. That all who come to prison do not avail themselves of the opportunities presented to change their former way of living, is true. There are many such, from many causes, that are not capable of being changed in their ways by any methods of teaching or direction by others. Education may be set down as one of the reasons why they do not alter their mode of living, being associated from birth with vice and immorality, with only the teaching and example of parents who were educated in the same sort of environment. Most of the hereditary crime-class people have schoolmasters' and book-learning, which by many who are engaged in the care of this class consider as quite sufficient means to prevent crime and to reclaim criminals.

Prison Labor.

NATIONAL PRISON ASSOCIATION, HELD AT ATLANTA, GA.,
NOVEMBER, 1886.

Upon the subject of Prison Labor Mr. Cassidy spoke as follows:

There is no difficulty about the system of individual treatment and work, and everything else, conducted as it is in the Eastern Penitentiary. It is the only public account system which there is in this country. There never was a contract made, from the time the corner-stone was laid. We don't like contractors; they are dangerous people to have around; they are always looking for percentages and "divvies." There are some reasons why intelligent industries are essential in any prison labor that requires both brain and muscle. The machinery labor of prisons is only an adjunct to the contractor, in order to produce largely. There is no intelligence connected with a machine, after it has left the hands of the man who invented it; it does not require any intelligence on the part of the operator. If prisoners are educated to labor with their hands and their heads, and are given the use of tools, and are allowed to go out in the community and take part with all other people who are laboring with the use of tools, very many of them do not come back to prison, for that very reason. The difficulty in managing so many people, and so many different industries, is not so great as it seems to those who do not know, or have had no experience in that way. Material can be purchased just as cheap by one man as another, if he has got the money to pay for it. Goods manufactured or made by hand are a better article, and on the market command more money than machine goods, and do not interfere with honest industry. Many men have large factories, purchase materials, manufacture goods, and put them on the market; and there is no reason why the State cannot employ suitable people for that purpose. I have plenty of time; I do not have half enough to do. I am complained of, because I am idle most of the time. It is no great exercise to send out a wagon loaded with goods, to have a man haul it out, send a bill for the goods, and get the money back. It doesn't require any great amount of labor to do that, nor much brains. I send goods all over the country. The best women's shoes in this town to-day are made in our prison; nobody complains of them; they do not interfere with trade. If Warden McClaughry will only consider how easy it would be to control this matter himself, he would never have a contractor come near his place if he could help it. You cannot make large returns; prisoners should not be made use of in that way. The best interest of the individual and of the prison, and the interest of the community outside, should be considered. When you do that, you do all that can be done for the prisoner and society.

We make women's and men's shoes very largely. They are all made by hand-labor. There is not a particle of power machinery in the place. We have one little engine there, for pumping water out of a well into the reservoir; that is all the power we have ever had. We made mats until the market for hand-made mats was destroyed by the cheaper machine-made in other prisons. We make cigars, cane-seat chairs, and hosiery; we use knitting machines, operated by hand, for manufacturing the hosiery.

WARDEN'S ANNUAL REPORT, 1895.

To find labor for convicts is a question that has puzzled prison authorities for years. The great objection of the community to have convict-made articles placed on the open market cripples any industry that may be introduced into prisons.

The political economist contends that the inmates of prisons should be self-supporting, which is a very just proposition. They do not indicate or suggest any method by which the desired end can be reached.

The large mass of the community, producers and consumers, also the transfer agents of production, which are known as business men, say that convict-made articles should not have equal standing in the general market.

Laws have been enacted by the proper State authority indorsing this view and prohibiting the sale of such products on equal terms. Commission men will not handle nor will traveling salesmen carry them, consequently the avenues for disposing of prison-made articles are practically closed under existing statutory restrictions. The remedy or relief for such a condition has not yet been found.

Testimony before Legislative Investigating Committee,

May 13, 1897.

Q.—How much employment is given a prisoner daily?

A.—About the ordinary amount that a man would do outside in four hours, when we have work for them. We haven't the work to keep them employed. We cannot get it.

Q.—Why?

A.—Trade is very dull now, and we have to go to a far-off market to sell the goods. We cannot sell them in Pennsylvania in consequence of the labor law.

Q.—What is your opinion of the effect upon the men, from keeping them employed more or less during the day?

A.—Employment is the best physical treatment you can give the men.

Q.—Has it not been apparent to you, from your observations, that if the men are not employed their condition deteriorates, both mentally and physically?

A.—I am not settled on that point. A great many of these people will not take any employment at all; they never did any work, but have subsisted on what other people earned. Idleness does not hurt them a bit, they grow fat on it.

Q.—Is that the experience you have had with the majority of the inmates?

A.—Yes, the only way they will work is by being paid for doing it, that is the only way they will work industriously. Then if there is no overwork on hand they will do their task slowly and always keep below the mark; but if you hold out the prospect of overwork, they will do their tasks, so as to do the overwork.   They will be industrious in order to get a little money.

Q.—Would it not be better for the State to submit to some little loss, rather than keep the inmates of this institution in idleness?

A.—No, I don't think the State can afford to lose money for any such reason.   If you can get a new dollar for an old one, it is all right, but you cannot satisfactorily explain a loss.

Q.—Then the State would lose less money by merely providing for their support than it would by having them employed in manufacturing operations which did not realize a profit?

A.—Yes, it would lose money very fast in the manufacturing business if it did not get back a dollar for every one it invested.

Q.—Have you up to the present time been able to get a new dollar for an old one?

A.—Always.   I have very seldom taken the risk of a loss.

Convict Contract Labor and Convict Earnings.

At the Meeting of the National Prison Association in New York in 1883.

When this question was under discussion, the president of the association requested Mr. Cassidy to give his views.   In compliance with this request, he said:

It was decided positively this morning that labor was essential in all prison management.   It is also essential to the welfare of every community.   All the greatness and all the wealth of every city is produced by its labor.   It is a great mistake in the jurists to make labor a penalty for crime, making labor offensive by degrading it in that way.   Labor as a punishment and labor as a duty are two different things.   In a prison, labor should not be used as a punishment, except in its application to the individual.   There are many individuals that labor would be irksome to.   There are quite a great many that labor is a blessing to.   Labor in a prison is only a punishment so far as it is applicable to the individual.   Regardless of any profit that may be derived from the product of the labor, it is of vast importance that it should be used as an auxiliary in the treatment of the individual.

In the community, the laborer—I don't care how hard the labor is, if he is carrying bricks and mortar to the top of a building, he does it cheerfully. When the building is done and the boss tells him he has no more work, he doesn't rejoice at that as being relieved of a punishment, but he goes and seeks labor elsewhere. The severest punishment we have in our prison is depriving the individual of labor. In the rarest cases, where prisoners will refuse to work, they are generally not level-headed entirely; there is something lacking about them; want of capacity to do work sometimes. It is one of the most difficult things to get the kind of labor that you can adapt to the people that you have. All the mechanical trades require a training. The way that labor is applied in our prison is to teach them some kind of occupation, and it requires time, and some have not the capacity for it. There are many people whom we try to make shoemakers of, and we find that they cannot do the work. Then we have to try them on some other grade of labor that we have, such as putting bottoms in cane chairs, which is simple. The profit derived from it is the secondary consideration to the treatment of the individual. That the trade should be of use to the individuals after they leave prison is of more importance than the profits while they are there.

I do not know what percentage of our men make use of their trades after they leave prison, because we cannot ascertain what they do or where they go. There are many I know in our own city who are following occupations that they learned in our prison. Two men who learned their trade in prison, I know, are carrying on the shoe-making business quite successfully, and are good, reputable citizens. We have no machinery. Machinery is no part of the learning of a trade. They sit down to work, and learn a trade in the old-fashioned way, out and out, each one. That requires time, and a loss of time while they are doing it. By the aid of machinery, in partnership with the manufacturer, you can convert your prison into a manufactory and have profitable results, I will admit.

The prisoners earn, on an average, about twelve cents a day, and the cost of maintenance, including all expenses, is about thirty-eight cents a day.

The trades that are most popular rarely get to prison. Out of our whole population of 1080 I believe there are but twelve men who have been trained to a mechanical business. Many of them have worked at trades in other prisons; some have worked part of the time and turned to vagabondism the other part. But of men who have been trained to business regularly as they were before the apprenticeship system was abolished,—shoemakers, carpenters, or machinists,—we have but twelve. The best mechanics become dissipated, get into houses of correction, sell everything they have, their tools and their clothes, go down to the lowest grade that humanity can come to, and then they brace up and go to work. They rarely get to the crime-class. When we have a man who can do good work in the crime-class, he has learned it in other prisons; whether it is cabinet-making or shoemaking, or any other work that is done, there is something about it that doesn't look like work turned out by a regular mechanic in the community; it has a prison look about it which a prison man who understands it will notice.

I am opposed to every form of congregating people in the crime-class. * * * The plan Mr. Brockway spoke of—he calls it the piece-price plan—we have used in the cotton-goods industries. It worked for a while and then failed.

Our prisoners earn about $40,000 a year, and $10,000 for themselves. Last year their overwork was about $10,000 in round figures, and that they dispose of as they think proper. Anything that will make the tie stronger between the prisoner and his family, and keep a place for him to go to when he goes out, is most beneficial.

We cane-seat chairs, employing as many as two hundred people generally, and just in accordance as the supply and demand require it. We manufacture chairs entirely out of the raw plank; we buy the lumber. That is an industry that requires some time to learn and some skill. We buy our own materials. We never had a contract since the corner-stone was laid for anything, provisions, supplies, material, labor, or in any way.

We do the best we can,—purchase the material and manufacture the goods. The goods we make are better standard, generally, than the same grade of goods in the market,—all hand-made; and we get a little more for shoes than the manufactory shoes bring. We have a hundred men making cigars; the largest amount is of cheap-grade cigars,—*some* fine ones. Once in a while we get a regular cigarmaker.

The largest amount of individual daily earnings is over seventy-five cents. The prisoner, for instance, is working at shoe-making, makes one pair and a half of shoes per day, at twenty cents a pair; that is thirty cents. Of all he makes over that half is credited to him and the other half to the county from which he came, at the same rates.   Some will make five, six, seven pairs of shoes a day.   Then the same with cigars.   They make 150 cigars; that amounts to thirty cents, and all over that they get the same price for.   The money they can give to their families or reserve it all until they go out.   I have known men on a five years' sentence to accumulate $250 to $300.   They work early and work late there. We have no particular hours for work.   They can work all the time they choose,—use their own time about doing it, eat their meals when they choose, read when they choose, between daylight and nine o'clock at night.   Some industrious men will work all the time in order to get some money for their families.   If a poor woman who has children and house rent to pay can get five or six dollars on the order of the prisoner, it makes a great deal for her and it keeps a home for the prisoner when he comes out.

At this point the members of the Prison Association submitted numerous questions, which are given with the answers by Mr. Cassidy.

Q.—What per cent. of your inmates are recommitted to your prison?

A.—I cannot give the percentage now.   The recommitments are more than we desire.   We keep a record of them and get them all, beyond any question.

Q.—What is the largest amount any prisoner ever earned?

A.—I paid a man that went out last Sunday $400, on a seven years' sentence.

Q.—Do you think that would act as an inducement to commit crime again?

A.—On the contrary, it gives them an opportunity to get away and into some business.   They can find employment without resorting to their old associates.

Q.—What is the expense per day of feeding your prisoners?

A.—About ten cents.   Those who have earned money rarely come back.   There is no greater incentive in life than what can be gained by honest industry, and every one in a community is in duty bound to do all that he can in whatever business he is engaged.   The man that *can* do the most work *ought* to do the most work always, and when you give him an opportunity in working for himself he will do all that he can.   In many cases certain men can do three times as much as those who are beside them without any effort at all. The State assumes control of the individual, and I do not think that it is fair for the State to shove any part of that responsibility on the irresponsible contractors who are not connected with the State government. The prisoners ought to be managed entirely by authority; and where you introduce outside people who have no authority, as in contract-labor prisons, where the contractors themselves are responsible to no one, and have no authority whatever, even if it is beneficial to the State in a remunerative way, it is not the best thing for the State to do. The State assumes control of these people when they are convicted, and the State ought to continue to control all their actions while they are in its charge.

As far as the prisoner has capacity to do so, he ought to be obliged to support himself, and so far as the demand to do so is applicable to the individual. Labor is not a punishment, except in its application to the individual. If you are benefiting him by fitting him to be a better citizen when he regains his freedom, you are accomplishing all that could be desired, and far greater benefit to the State than the few dollars he may earn, if it is divided between the State and an irresponsible person.

Q.—How are you going to determine how much work he shall do?

A.—By studying his capacity.

Q.—Some men won't work unless you compel them?

A.—They are few.

Q.—It is also possible to increase a man's capacity for work by thorough training?

A.—That is true; yes. In working for so much apiece, when he increases his capacity he is benefiting himself. Men will at first think it is an impossibility to make what is required of the general class; after awhile they will be surprised at themselves to see how much they can do. There are a great many people who go to prisons who have no capacity for anything. not from any desire to avoid doing what you require them to do; but we try them at different things, and they have no capacity for doing anything at all.

Q.—Would you compel a man to work who does not want to?

A.—I would try that; yes, sir.

Q.—Then, in his case, labor becomes a punishment?

A.—To that man, yes.

Q.—Do you propose to divide the earnings of that man the same as with a man who does his work willingly?

A.—If he earns it, yes.

Q.—Then you punish him and make him pay for his own punishment?

A.—And if he destroys his materials we make him pay for them. We treat him precisely as we would a mechanic in any private business. If he destroys the materials or tools we deduct it from his wages; that is done in all business. The labor of prisons is one of the problems that is agitating the people of New York more, I suppose, perhaps, than any other subject. I do not know practically the workings of the contract-labor system, because I have never had any experience in it, only what I have read and seen.

Q.—You favor a public account as against the contract system?

A.—Precisely. The State ought to be capable of managing its own affairs, and of managing every department that belongs to the State; it presumes to do that in all other departments of the State. It is a large corporation, and it should be entirely responsible to its people for what it does. A prison management can be conducted just as well as an individual management anywhere else.

Q.—Then the argument that the contract system is good because it requires a low grade of capacity in administration is practically against it?

A.—Yes. A large manufacturing interest of any kind,—take Singer's sewing-machine concern, or any other similar institution, —is managed by individuals trained and selected for the purpose. There is no reason why the State cannot go to the expense of training people to care for its interests just as well as a corporation can. The way it is at our prison, the warden is elected every six months; if he is a bad man six months is long enough.

Q.—You have been there how many years?

A.—Twenty-five years. If he is a good man it is no trouble to re-elect him. The State cannot be at any disadvantage. * * * The State can be responsible for all its people.

Q.—How many men do you work in your prison on a daily average?

A.—Sometimes we have 800 or 900; just as we have work for them.

Q.—Do you have a daily average of 500?

A.—Yes; over that.

Q.—And you earn $40,000?

A.—Yes.

Q.—Your earnings are not in proportion to the earnings in the contract-labor system?

A.—No, sir; and they cannot be. With the advantage of machinery, and of the manufacturer that is in partnership with the machinery, they can work all kinds of men.

Q.—Can you refer to any time when the State has assumed all this management and has made a success of it?

A.—A pecuniary success? Yes. There is no prison population that can be made pecuniarily a success to any great extent, however. It may be made in prosperous times to pay expenses, if it is located just where there is a particular kind of labor that they can do. The House of Correction at Allegheny was a success financially, owing to the fact that it was opened at a time, and located where there was an industry in active demand,—oil barrels. That was all that they did; if the oil barrel demand should stop, the House of Correction would stop.

Q.—What is the difference between the two systems of prison labor in its moral effect upon the prisoner?

A.—To begin with, the contract has to be attended to by the contractor to secure his personal interest in it. He has to employ a large number of citizens, who go in and associate with the convicts, and which has not a good moral tendency.

Q.—Wouldn't you have to do this under any system?

A.—No, sir; there is no such necessity when the prison is managed by what you term a public-account system. You can make the goods for so much, and you must have officers capable of directing the labor.

Q.—Do you have instructors?

A.—Our officers are the instructors. The officers are trained to their business in the beginning. They are employed in the lower grades as night watchmen or as mechanics for some time in the general branches of business. We select some one from these night watchmen to fill a vacancy that may occur in the shoe or chair-making or cane departments. The officers are never changed except for cause, or if they choose to quit, but that is seldom. There is no one from the outside that can come in.

There is no prison that can be well managed in any way where any outsider can come between the authority and the prison. A prison government, to be a proper government, must be a one-man government, and no outside influence can come in between the officer and the people he has charge of, only in a general supervisory way,—as those who have authority to visit; but everything must go through one man.

Q.—If the Supervisory board interferes it does not harm?

A.—That is very different from others who visit the prison. All matters must go through the hands of the overseer who has charge of the prisoners, in order to give the understanding that everything received must be received directly from the overseer, and nothing can be brought in by any one else. The overseer is held responsible for the people in his charge.

Q.—How would it be possible, under the congregate plan, to work the men in prison without instructors?

A.—The State can employ instructors just as well as a contractor can.

In conclusion, I would say that the Eastern Penitentiary has long ceased to be an experiment. It has been in operation now fifty-four years. This is a sufficiently long time to dispel any idea that it is merely an experiment. It has been conducted on this plan from the beginning.

Insane Prisoners.

From Warden's Annual Report, 1890.

In years gone past, one of the objections made to the cellular system, as it was then called, was, it was likely to impair the mind of the persons under its treatment. That theory has been abandoned long since for want of facts. There are insane people in all prisons, and more in proportion than in the same number of the community at large, for many of the crimes committed are such that only insane persons would conceive.

Many of the reports of prisons this year refer to the care of insane criminals and the proper disposition of them so earnestly, that insane prisoners are found in many of the congregate prisons. Some advocate their removal to insane hospitals when the disease is positively developed; others advocate the construction of separate prisons for insane criminals. New York has such an institution. A separate prison for insane prisoners would be the proper disposition of that class, but they should not be sent there until their term of sentence had expired, or sent there direct from the court upon conviction. As soon as it is known in a prison that the insane can be removed before the expiration of sentence, there will be much simulating in order to get to a hospital, as escape would be considered easier than from the prison proper. Simulated insanity is more trouble to the officers of the prison than real insanity.

Separation of the classes that make up the prison population is the common sense of the subject. There is a class in all prisons in considerable numbers that it would be proper to provide a separate prison for,—persons who are convicted of crimes against persons where property was in no way connected with the offense. They are not criminals, nor are they likely to be after the expiration of the term of which they were sentenced. They are generally the best-conducted prisoners in any prison. Many of them convicted of the crime for which they were sentenced were innocent of any intent to commit crime before or at the time of its commission, and frequently had no knowledge of it for some time after. Most of this class are industrious. Honest and truthful, generally respected by the community in which they lived, they do not require the treatment necessary for the habitual criminal. A separate prison for this class is as much needed as for the criminal insane.

From Warden's Annual Report, 1892.

The increase of insane inmates in the various institutions in this State for the care and treatment of such persons is greater than the increase of the criminal population of the State. Insane persons convicted of crime are generally committed to the prisons. Juries hesitate to find verdicts of murder in the first degree when insanity, real or simulated, is offered as the defense. Objections are made to having insane persons in prisons; to have persons convicted of crime sent to the hospitals which the State has provided for the treatment of such of its citizens so afflicted is also objectionable. An institution in a central location, with two separate departments, one for all the criminal insane and the other for all persons convicted of homicide of a lesser degree than that to which capital punishment is awarded,—such an institution would relieve both the penitentiaries and the State hospitals for the insane of persons, who could be treated more carefully and much safer for themselves and others.   Out of the whole number (1104) in this Penitentiary on the the first of January, 106 were convicted of homicide, the defense in many of these cases being insanity.

Insanity.

TESTIMONY BEFORE LEGISLATIVE COMMITTEE, AT THE PENITEN-
TIARY, JUNE 21, 1897.

Q.—Is the simulating of insanity common or rare in prisons, as compared with the same thing in persons on the outside?

A.—The motive in the prison is far greater than it is among the generality of the community outside.   The simulators in a prison are a class of people that are not exactly like any class outside in this respect, that those outside are not attacked or show symptoms in the same way so much.

Q.—I wish you would give us the benefit of your experience, stating individual instances, in regard to the motives that induce prisoners to practice deception, and to what lengths the prisoner will go, also the arts they will practice or engage in to play the part of a lunatic?

A.—They will resort to almost any suffering and torture before they will give it up, and some don't give it up at all, but continue it during their entire time here.   I knew of one man who was here, who it was admitted by everybody in the place, had lost his teeth, and could not talk, and that he had a suicidal mania.   But he always managed to hang himself just before the overseer was coming along to serve the dinner, shut the door, or do something, when the man would be pretty sure to be discovered before he would choke.   He continued that for five years.   They couldn't trap him.   If a slate was handed to him, he would write on it.   He finally got a pardon.   When he came down to the office to leave, he could talk as well as I do now; he could talk elegantly.

Q.—Do they or not frequently exhibit a marvellous cunning notwithstanding a very limited intelligence?

A.—Yes, most of the mentally-affected or feeble-minded people exhibit great ingenuity.   One woman who was here,—had been several times before,—had a trouble called "galvanic rheumatism." She couldn't walk, but had to go on crutches. She fooled her three years' sentence in that way. She then complained at another time of some internal trouble, and called the doctor for treatment. When leaving the institution, as soon as she reached the outside, she flung the crutches inside.

Q.—When a prisoner confesses that he has been playing and makes a full acknowledgment, is he treated thereafter the same as other prisoners, or are privileges, such as books, writing letters, etc., withheld from him?

A.—He is treated just precisely the same as he was when he commenced it, or just where he left off. No matter what he has done, if he has assaulted an officer, and badly injured him, the prisoner receives the same sort of treatment he received before the commission. I would like it to be distinctly understood that there is not one particle of vengeance in this institution, and never has been.

Q.—When prisoners suddenly break out in a frenzy or exhibit the slightest mental disturbance, what is done, or what means are employed to arrive at an intelligent opinion, to guide you in the disposal of a particular case or in the treatment of it?

A.—To get the prisoner by himself and treat him in that way, individually, until we can ascertain something about the case. You cannot do it when he has some one with him to encourage him. Once I have made up my mind the man is insane I always promptly inform the Judge sending him here.

Q.—Does it happen that Judges send you prisoners who are insane on reception, instead of sending them to an insane asylum? If so, does this not tend to lead the public to form unwarranted conclusions respecting the treatment of prisoners?

A.—Yes, it has been stated in evidence here that no Judge had sent here a prisoner who was insane. Last week a Judge of our court here sentenced a lunatic for fifteen years, and didn't send him to an insane asylum, but sent him to prison.

Q.—Can you recall any cases where the prisoners, as the result of care and treatment given them, regained their former health and were discharged in as good a condition as they were when received?

A.—There are many cases of that sort, cases in which the Commission have decided that the prisoners ought to be removed, where the prisoners have gotten well and gone out.

The Bertillon System for the Registration of Prisoners.

NATIONAL PRISON ASSOCIATION, TORONTO, CANADA, SEPTEMBER 12, 1887.

Upon the proposition to adopt the Bertillon System for the Registration of Prisoners, Mr. Cassidy made these observations:

Society is entitled to some protection in spite of all the sentimentalism of theorists. The professional burglar who enters houses in the middle of the night may not commit murder. But in all cases of burglary human life is put in jeopardy. And often where a delicate wife or daughter is at home, the happiness of the family is ruined by nervous prostration resulting from excitement. Yet society is advised to take the scoundrel who wrought this mischief and handle him delicately and protect him. Honest people have a right to protection as well as burglars. Three offenses should have capital penalties attached to them: burglary by night where human life is endangered, the obstruction of a railroad, and arson. Then there will be no need of registration. The community is saved the expense of recommitment. It is better to dispose of such men in this way than it is to lock them up for ten or fifteen years, to be cared for and preached at and the Gospel forced upon them without effect. Commutation laws are made for this class of criminals. A professional criminal, the moment he enters prison, begins to calculate the time he can earn by good behavior, and he gains every minute of it. The poor fellow who never saw the inside of a prison before, loses his temper and his good time with it. He is not posted as is the man who makes crime a business.

The first effort of a habitual criminal is to square himself with the policeman by whom he is arrested. Next he tries to get bail at the preliminary hearing before the magistrate. Then, through friends, he endeavors to keep witnesses away from the grand jury. Failing in these several stages, he secures the best lawyer his means will permit, and then begins a legal tussle before the court and jury, where every device is taken advantage of to postpone trial or accomplish a miscarriage of justice. Those who are unfortunate enough to miss all these avenues of escape, and finally get inside of prison doors, continue to use every influence they can reach to make their time easier, through special favors from prison authorities or by their own exemplary conduct as prisoners earning the largest possible commutation for good behavior. Every official connected in any way with the search for, arrest, trial, and imprisonment of these criminals knows well of the almost innumerable methods adopted to escape justice, and how frequently they are in whole or in part successful—I speak of the professional criminal—knows in advance just what chances he takes and is prepared to act.

All these avenues of escape society opens to the criminal, and it costs time and money to place the most dangerous criminals behind the bars.

Something ought to be done for the community.

Do any of you get a reward for behaving yourselves? Every good citizen behaves himself without being rewarded for it. The sympathy of the community is with the vagabond in prison. It demands of the warden that he shall allow the prisoner every privilege to which he may be entitled by the law; but if merited punishment is inflicted upon a disobedient inmate, then there is a public outcry against inhumanity.

At the National Prison Association, at Pittsburg, Pa., October 10–14, 1891, Warden Cassidy read the following paper:

Prisons I Visited in Ireland, England, France, and Belgium, and What I Saw—1890.

MR. PRESIDENT AND GENTLEMEN OF THE PRISON WARDENS' ASSOCIATION OF THE UNITED STATES:

Not being present at the last annual meeting of the Association held in September, 1890, at Cincinnati, some explanation is demanded by the President, who will not accept excuses or apologies, but must have facts that will justify non-attendance. I will state the cause of my absence from the last meeting and give the facts.

An *alibi* is a good defense in any case, if you really have one, and I think I have.

Lord Lytton said, "That a dunce who has been to Rome excels a dunce that stayed at home."

On the 21st of June, 1890, I took passage on the good ship "Ethiopia," which sailed from New York on that date, bound for Glasgow, via Londonderry; at twelve noon passed Sandy Hook lightship, ten miles. I was then fairly out of the jurisdiction of the United States, on a British ship, and under the English flag.

The voyage was devoid of any particlar incident, as most sea voyages are. In eleven days we were landed in Londonderry, Ireland, on the 1st of July, at 10 P.M.

My first desire next morning was to see the jail. I waited on Mayor Baxter and presented letters from Mayor Fitler and Director of Police Stokley, of Philadelphia. I was received very courteously and my request to visit the jail complied with.

THE JAIL AT LONDONDERRY.

The mayor accompanied me to the jail, where he introduced me to the chief officer in charge, the governor being absent. The chief warder (subordinate officers are styled warders) escorted me through the prison, which is an old structure, the ground plan of which is a semicircle, or more plainly described, like a horseshoe.

The cell structure is three tiers high, containing one hundred and fifty cells. The cells are seven by ten feet by nine feet high, lighted by window two feet by twenty inches cross-barred, making it secure and admitting sufficient light and air. The doors of the cells open on a passage about six feet wide running on the outside of the circle. Each cell has close wooden doors secured by locks and bolts, with vision holes in the doors for supervision. The cell furniture consists of a wooden form two feet wide, six feet long, with sides like a box, which raises it seven inches from the floor. No bed, two blankets, two sheets, no pillow, a mess pan, tin cup, no knives or forks, a bench to sit on, no water in the cells only as brought in. The diet is sufficient, but the food not plenty. The structure is an old one; part of it was built in the seventeenth century; the most recent additions were made about eighty years ago.

There were forty female prisoners in a separate building, cared for by a matron, with three assistants.

There are twenty officers employed, who are paid about $500 per annum. These officers are armed with pistols.

There appears to be very good supervision, but no productive labor done other than breaking stone for contractors who make streets. The price paid is ten pence per ton, twenty cents of our money.

All supplies are purchased by contract, given out by the government. Cost *per diem per capita* one shilling and eight pence, forty-one cents of our money.

The entrance to the jail is through a gateway about ten feet wide; an outer wooden gate with a wicket-gate to admit persons. At the inner end of the gateway, which is about sixty feet, is an iron latticed gate, the gate-keepers, and receiving office between the two gates. This is the only entrance to the jail.

The ventilation appears to be free, as no perceptible odor is noticeable in passing through the prison.

The prisoners have an hour of walking exercise each day, walking about ten feet apart, and are not permitted to communicate, and subject to some penalty if they are observed doing so. They are not masked or covered in any way to prevent recognition.

Most of the inmates are young men with sentences of two years down to thirty days. No negroes. Only one death in each of the past two years.

The washing of prisoners' clothes is done by the female inmates of the jail. Some of the women are engaged picking oakum, which is a punishment surely.

There are very strict regulations in regard to the admission of visitors. No person is admitted unless by official order of one of the visiting justices, or the mayor, who is one by virtue of his office.

Prisoners are permitted to have visits from friends once in three months and allowed to write every two months.

Tobacco is prohibited. There is a library, but it is very limited.

The general public are not permitted to visit the prison.

They have Protestant and Catholic service on Sundays. The Catholic priest visits the prisoners during the week. The separate system of treatment is observed as the primary discipline of the management.

My visit to the Derry jail was very interesting, and having seen all of it I bid good-bye to Derry.

Next day, July 4th, I went to Belfast; arrived there that evening. Next morning went out to see about getting into the Antrim County Jail, located there. The mayor was not at the mayor's office. I went to his place of business at Linen Hall; was there informed that the mayor was out of town. His clerk after some trouble obtained an order from one of the visiting justices admitting me into the

ANTRIM COUNTY PRISON.

It is the most complete county prison I have ever seen, built of brown stone, covering nearly ten acres. Double gateway, with the governor's residence on the right, inside of the gate. The order of admission was sent to the governor by the gate-keeper, and was returned with directions to give me in charge of the chief warder. All subordinate officers of prisons here are termed warders. The governor did not make his appearance. The chief warder was entirely familiar with all the details of the prison and its management. He gave me every opportunity to see all of the workings of the institution.

There are four blocks of cells, three tiers high, running off from one center, with cells on either side of a ten-foot hallway.

There are seven hundred cells in all, six feet six inches in width by twelve feet in length, ten feet high, lighted by a barred window two feet by twenty inches, closed wooden doors locked on the outside, a small opening in the door for supervision. The cell floors are of concrete. They have gas-light in each cell. No water or water-closet. Not much furniture of any sort. The bed arrangement much the same as in the Derry Jail; a box for a bed, which stands on end during the day, with blankets folded on top. In the yard there are stalls six feet in width, about eight feet in depth, roofed over with the front open. There is no productive labor other than breaking stone, except some shoemaking and weaving for the use of the prison.

These stalls are built in ranges; one prisoner is placed in each stall to keep them separate. A tramway runs along the open end of the stalls. The stone is brought to them, and when broken taken away on this tramway. Each prisoner has an allotted amount to do, which can be done easily in the time allowed. The stone is used in making streets.

There are two hundred and forty women in a separate building, cared for by female attendants.

All the washing for the prison is done by the women.

There were six hundred prisoners in confinement at that time, in charge of thirty male and ten female subordinate officers. There are fifty officers of all grades employed.

The term of sentence to this prison is mostly for six months and less.

Everything is in good order and clean.

In the inclosure between the cell buildings is a set of yards for separate exercise. Eight separate inclosures radiating from a center where there is an elevated observatory, in which is placed an officer for supervision of the prisoners during the time of exercise. These yards are in an octagon space, with walls separating each prisoner. Separate or cellular treatment is carried out entirely— no congregating of prisoners for any purpose. In chapel the seats are partitioned so that the prisoners do not mingle. Both Catholic and Protestant service is held every Sunday.

There is so much formality in the discipline that there is little time for any one thing.

The cooking is done in the basement and the cooked food sent up on elevators.

For ventilation there is a shaft or chimney one hundred feet high. There is a flue running along in the inner wall near the top of the cells, leading into the shaft, with openings from each cell into the flue, which takes off any foul air that may be in the cells. There is a fire constantly kept in the bottom of the shaft which creates a strong draught continuously, insuring a constant current of air through the cells. There is no perceptible odor in any part of the prison.

The inside walls are whitewashed. The corridors are lighted by large skylights in the roof.

This prison has been in use about thirty years. The separate or cellular method of treatment has been strictly observed from the first. The architecture of the structure is taken from the Eastern State Penitentiary at Philadelphia. The method pursued in the treatment of the individuals therein confined is the same as is known everywhere in Europe as the Pennsylvania system.

Thanking the chief warder for his kind attention and his evident desire to give me every opportunity to see all of the prison, I bade him good-bye.

After leaving the prison I took a conveyance and was shown much of Belfast and its suburbs, which are extensive. Wide streets, fine residences, large business places, public buildings, colleges, churches, parks, botanical gardens, all evidencing thrift and industry in the people of Belfast.

After spending several days in the mountains of Donegal and Derry I went to Dublin. Next morning after arriving there I went to Dublin Castle to find some authority that would admit me into the prison located there.   I was directed to the prison board that direct the management of convict prisons of Ireland.   I saw the vice-president of the board, presented a letter from Richard Vaux, president of the board of inspectors of the Eastern State Penitentiary.   Vice-President O'Brien read the letter.   He said, "I know of this gentleman; his name is sufficient guarantee for anything in my power to grant."   He gave me an order of admission to the governor of the

Mount Joy Prison,

which is considered the model institution of the Irish system.   The prison is about twenty minutes' ride from the center of the city, very pleasantly located, covering about nine acres.   On presenting the order at the gate I was taken in charge by the deputy-governor, the governor being absent at the time.   I was given every opportunity to see all of the conduct and management of the prison.

The structure of this prison is similar to the one at Belfast. Three blocks of cells radiate from an octagon center.   They are three tiers high, with cells on either side of a ten-foot corridor. There are six hundred cells in all.   The dimensions of the cells are the same as cells in the County Antrim Jail.   Cell furniture consists of a table and stool chained together, and a box with sides four inches high, six feet long, twenty inches wide.   This box swings across the cell on hooks when in use, about eighteen inches from the floor.   A thin mattress, two blankets and a rug cover are provided.   This sort of bed is for the orderly class who are well conducted and have been in prison more than a year; all others have blankets but no mattress.   The box·stands on end against the wall during the day with the bed clothes on top neatly folded.   A tin basin, tin water cup, tin mess pan, are the total of the prisoner's conveniences.   No ornament of any sort permitted in any of the cells.   The food is limited and given in quantity according to the class of the prisoner.   Half pound of meat cooked away in soup twice a week; the meat is weighed before cooked.   Oatmeal mush other days.   One pint of soup is the ration; that is all one can have; coffee or gruel for breakfast and supper.

There is no productive or skilled labor other than a limited amount of mats and some matting, which is sold in the city.   All other work done is for the prison.   Clothes and shoes are made for this and other prisons. All building, mason, and carpenter work is done by the inmates, and it is well done.

There is no overwork, but there is a gratuity allowed and given on discharge; this gratuity is forfeited by misconduct any time during the term of the prisoner.

There are ten dark or punishment cells radiating from a center. They have double doors and a vestibule to each cell of about four feet square. The door of the vestibule opens into the center, the cell door opens into the vestibule. These cells are about four feet wide at the door, widening as they extend back to eight feet at the rear end; they are about twelve feet in length. They are lighted from skylight in the roof, but can be made absolutely dark. These cells are fifteen feet high. They are dungeons surely.

No seasoning is furnished to the prisoner for the food, such as salt, pepper, or vinegar; he must take it as prepared.

I saw all of this prison and talkel with the chief warder and other officers about the characteristics of the people who make up the population of the prison. I find that the inmates of Irish penal institutions have the same peculiarities as those confined elsewhere under similar conditions.

The management of the Mount Joy Prison is conducted on the Pennsylvania system of non-association of prisoners.

The ticket-of-leave system in Ireland—parole it is called in the United States—has not produced the results that Captain Maconochie and Sir Walter Crofton, the projectors, and other advocates of the system expected to be derived from it. Originally, according to methods pursued in carrying it out, a convict having a twelve-years' sentence would serve eight months at the Mount Joy Prison. Then transferred to Spike Island, a congregate prison, to serve at least seven years. He may then be liberated on license after serving nine years altogether. That license is the parole. Spike Island Prison has been abandoned altogether. Time served there was considered the most important feature in the Irish system. The police surveillance of released prisoners is still maintained, the results of which, in a country governed as Ireland is, makes emigration the only alternative for the discharged prisoner. By this method the population of Irish prisons has been reduced, which fact has been frequently referred to as the results of the reformatory influence produced by the Irish system of parole and voluntary transportation.

There is no doubt of the efficiency of the management and direction of the discipline of the Mount Joy Prison. I went from there with pleasant recollections of the cordial attention shown me by the officer in charge and others connected with the institution.

Most of the inmates of the Irish prisons are young men under twenty-five years of age, and are apparently healthy. They look as if they were under a continual strain. The discipline is rigid and exacting, and must be enforced as the law directs. All the movements are precise as machinery. The garb worn by the prisoner is uniform in color and distinctive, but no stripes.

The cost *per diem per capita* one shilling and eight pence, about forty-one cents of our money. All expenditure is by government, and supplies furnished by contract.

From Dublin I went to the city of Cork, then to Queenstown by way of the Lakes of Killarney and Blarney Castle. All the points of interest on this route have been described by many tourists. Queenstown is a beautiful harbor. From the heights back of the town a fine view is had of the harbor and fortifications. Spike Island is situated in this harbor, directly opposite the town, on which can be seen the ruins of the famous prison which once constituted two-thirds of the parole system of Sir Walter Crofton. I returned to Dublin from Queenstown by way of Limerick. After spending several days looking around the beautiful city I left for London, feeling assured that an American is given the right of way anywhere in Ireland.

I left Dublin at 7 A.M. by boat from Kingstown to Holyhead; was four hours in crossing. From there took train, arrived in London at 5.30 P.M. Next morning I went to see about getting into the prisons. I first went to Scotland Yard, the police headquarters. Was there informed that they could do nothing, as the authority I required was vested entirely in the home office. I then went to the American Embassy, 123 Victoria Street, Westminster, where I was kindly received by Mr. White, secretary of Legation, to whom I presented my letters of identification. After looking them over he presented me to the American minister, Robert Lincoln, who was very kind and courteous, without any assumption of dignity or reserve. I was received and treated as an American citizen by an American gentleman.

He stated that he would make a request to the home department to have my application to visit the prisons favorably considered, and send me the reply of the home department when received.

It was several days before I received the orders that would admit me into the prisons. While waiting I saw much of London.

The first prison I went to when I received permission to do so was Millbank, which is situated on the river about two miles from the Charing Cross Hotel, where I was located.

On presenting the order of admission at the gate I was admitted to await the governor's direction. After waiting an hour for the governor I was taken in charge by the chief warder, who introduced me into the

MILLBANK PRISON.

It is an ill-contrived structure, not at all suited for the purpose for which it was designed, a separate treatment prison. It is dark and cheerless. The cells are six by twelve, nine feet high. The whole structure is of brick, not plastered. The prison is used as a lock-up or place of detention for persons awaiting trial.

This once great prison that was erected for a separate system prison, and was much boasted of at the time, has been a miserable failure, and the purpose for which it was constructed abandoned.

There is no work of any sort. The prisoners sent here are for short terms, not over three months.

No furniture in the cells, plank bed, three blankets, washbasin, and water can. There are no conveniences whatever for the prisoners.

Having seen all that I desired, bade the warder good-bye, I was met by the governor as I was going out. He is a tall, pleasant-looking gentleman, but had no time to waste on me, excused himself and went about his business, and I went my way.

There was nothing about Millbank Prison that would indicate that it had ever been suitable for a penal institution. I next went to the

PENTONVILLE PRISON.

On presenting the order for my admission into the prison I was handed over to the warder-in-chief, the governor not being visible. I was taken through the principal parts of the structure.

There are four blocks four tiers high radiating from one center, with cells on either side of a ten-foot wide corridor. The cells are of the same dimension as in the Irish prisons. From the center a general supervision is had of the whole.

This is the model prison of England, known as a penal servitude convict prison. Prisoners sentenced to five years or more are sent here. For the first nine months solitary confinement, and *it is* solitary.

Some work is done here, such as mat-making and clothes and shoes for prisoners and officers, but no productive labor. There are two large tread-wheels on which one hundred men can operate, making power sufficient to grind grain for making the flour used in the prison.

The men tramp on the wheel fifteen minutes, then a rest of five minutes, leaving two-thirds of the whole number on the wheel all the time. The wheel is about fifteen feet in diameter, with steps ten inches apart on the outside of the wheel, the weight of the men turning it. The weight of the men is always on the center of the outside of the wheel. They are continually climbing almost perpendicular, the wheel receding from them ten inches at every step they make. No doubt it is exercise; that is all the men get out of it.

The flour is not bolted, but made into bread whole as it comes from the stone, dark and coarse.

The food is prepared in the usual way and served in the cells. The soup is made with half pound of cooked meat and pease. The meat is cooked away in the soup, a pint of which is allowed to each prisoner. This ration is given twice a week. Other days porridge and suet pudding are provided.

The bread and everything is carefully weighed out. All get the same quantity. If a piece of bread is cut short of weight another piece is tacked on to it with a wooden peg. The diet is regulated by act of Parliament. The prisoner that requires more cannot get it. The one who does not want as much must take it. Everything is done by rule made by law, and must be complied with. No individual judgment of an officer is permitted in any case. They have dark cells for the refractory, and use irons and other mechanical restraints.

This structure was erected in 1840, and designed for a separate or cellular prison. The ground plan is taken from the Philadelphia prison.

All the prisons in this country are built of brick, not plastered, but whitewashed. Between the blocks or cell buildings are exercising grounds, where the prisoners have an hour each day, except Sunday or stormy weather. The men who have work do not have this exercise. There are not many of them.

They have a chapel for daily religious service as well as Sunday.

The officer who had me in charge seemed desirous of showing the chapel.

They have both Catholic and Protestant service on Sunday, and have both sorts of chaplains employed. Each prisoner is allowed to take his choice, and does so just as he finds the chaplain to suit his purpose, or the one he thinks he can the more easily impose on.

The clothes of the prisoners are washed in the general laundry. They consist of cotton shirt and drawers, woolen clothes if ordered by the doctor. The clothes after being washed are sent to the block from which they came and distributed promiscuously. There are eight hundred inmates. A prisoner may not have the same clothes twice during his term unless by accident. Knives and forks are not in use, as they are not required. The system of ventilation is by flues leading to a shaft. Sewer-drainage from the cells was abandoned, and a convenience at the end of each tier of cells substituted. The occupants of the cells on each tier must be taken to this convenience.

The Pentonville Prison is considered one of the best constructed and the best conducted in England.

I had not the pleasure of seeing the governor. Governors of the prisons of England are very exclusive gentlemen, appearing only on great occasions.

The chief warder is the man who has the routine and detail of the interior management of the prison.

All supplies are furnished by contract by government.

The prison officers are appointed by authority of the home office, and liable to be transferred to any other prison in the country. It is a regular service and continuous, the same as the police, subject to removal only by the department that appoints them.

One warder to ten prisoners is the regulation by law, exclusive of the staff officers, governors, doctors, and clerks, which are numerous.

The cell buildings were when erected three tiers high. An additional story has been added, making them four stories high.

The whole structure covers about seven and one-half acres. Military guard the inclosure.

The chief warder, who had me in charge, was very kind and obliging. He was very willing that I should see and understand all of the management. He knows all the details. Having put in all the time I could spare on one institution, bade the warder good-bye, I next went to the

Holloway Local Prison,

a neat structure on the radiating plan. It is a modern structure with three blocks of cells three tiers high. It is known as the Holloway Prison. None but short-term convicts are sent there. The cells are of the same dimensions as the other prisons visited, with light and ventilation the same. I next went to the prison

Wormwood-scrubs,

situated sixteen miles out of the city. This is a penal servitude or convict prison, and is considered as the most improved prison structure yet erected in England.

On presenting my order of admission I was taken in charge by the chief warder. He has been in the prison service twenty-eight years. I was shown everything that was of any interest. The warder was very anxious that I should see and understand all of the methods of treatment and the management.

There are three cell buildings finished and occupied. These structures run parallel with each other, about two hundred feet apart. They are four tiers high, of brick, with cells on each side of a twelve-foot wide corridor. The cell rooms and furniture about the same as in the other prisons, lighted and ventilated in the same way.

No general supervision can be had of the interior of these buildings, as they do not connect only by a covered passage-way running across the front end of the structures.

I went through two of the blocks. They have dark, or pun-ishment, cells that were constructed for the purpose, and are adapted for it. They have irons, hand-cuffs and shackles, and a triangle and cat, for corporal punishment. There is a place where all the implements used for punishment of prisoners are kept ready for use, known as the chain room. There are long chains to which a number of prisoners are fastened when being transferred from one penal institution to another. All convict prisons have the same facilities for enforcing disclipline and transferring prisoners.

The officers are armed with a short sword when on duty with any number of prisoners out of their cells. They have also police batons or clubs. No productive labor or work that required any skill was being done in this prison. Much of the work of erecting the buildings was performed by convicts drafted from the other penal servitude prisons.

After seeing all that was to be seen in that prison, and having seen all that I cared to see of the English and Irish prisons, I looked about London several days, visited Scotland Yard, was kindly received by Mr. Jarvis, an officer in that service, whose acquaintance I made when he was in Philadelphia on business a short time ago.

Before leaving London I called on William Tatlack, secretary of the Howard Association. He has been engaged on the philanthropic side of prison matters for a number of years and is well informed on the subject of treatment of criminals. He is fully convinced that the individual method of treating persons convicted of crime produces better results to the individual convict and society than any other known method. He asked many questions about American prisons and prison officials. He considers Captain Joseph Nicholson, President of this Wardens' Association, the ablest prison manager in America.

The physical condition of the inmates of English prisons is looked after carefully by those having charge of them, for insane, epileptic, or those who likely would do themselves harm especially. There is a cell heavily padded or upholstered, in which such cases are placed. The terms to be served in any of the prisons here are short, mostly less than a year, before they are transferred. Not much can be known of the individual characteristics of any number of them. The health of the prisoners, it is assumed, cannot be impaired by the length of term served in these prisons.

The officer, when asked, said that the death-rate was very small, as when a prisoner was ill and likely to die the home office procured his release.

Not more than two or three died in a year in the prison. The direction of all prisons in England is the same. All matters in reference to prisons and their management emanates from the home office. All records of each prison go to the home department.

After looking around London several days, seeing much that was interesting, I went to Paris by way of Folkestone and Boulogne. It is an hour's ride by rail from London to Folkestone. Then by boat across the straits of Dover to France; the trip across is made in an hour and a half. Then by rail to Paris. Arrived in Paris at 6.30 P.M.

Next morning went out to look around and call on Mr. Henry Pionneau, to whom I had letters of introduction. He received me kindly, and placed himself entirely at my service while I remained in Paris. He is a gentleman retired from business, speaks English, and has plenty of leisure time. Next day he came and directed me where I desired to go. I waited on the American Consul and obtained a letter of introduction to the Minister of the Interior, who has control of all the prisons in France.

I waited on the Minister of the Interior and presented letter from the consul; was very courteously received. He was desirous to further my request. He gave me an official order of admission to all the prisons that I desired to see and others that he wished me to see. He gave me his card, and invited me to call on him at his residence that evening. The order of admission included M. Pionneau, who accompanied me as interpreter. We first went to the

Madras Prison.

On presenting the minister's letter I was admitted at once. The chief officer here is entitled Director. That gentleman received us very kindly. This prison is an old one, erected in 1840. Has six blocks of cells, each block three tiers high, inclosed by a wall twenty-five feet high. There are nine hundred cells in all. The cells are six feet six inches by twelve feet, nine feet high, built of brick, and plastered. The walls are painted in two colors. Not much furniture in the cells; coarse woolen clothes, wooden shoes, The cells are lighted by window in the rear. There is sewerage from each cell; no supply of water in the cells. The refuse empties into a cask in the basement of the corridor, where there is a cask for each cell. These casks are emptied every twenty days. The cellar or tunnel under the corridor where these casks stand forms a conduit through which air is forced by a large fan through the pipes leading from the cells to these casks. Through the soil pipes the foul air is forced out of the conduit, much of it finding its way into the cells. This cellar or tunnel is a great nuisance. I was all through the underground part of the structure, and examined the method of sewerage. There has been no improvement made in this matter since the erection of the structure.

The construction of this prison is on the radiating plan, and is exclusively a cellular prison. One year is the maximum term of sentence to be served in this prison. After that the prisoner is sent to another place to serve the remainder of his sentence in a congregate prison, or is transported to New Caledonia.

The food is not abundant, and of a poor quality. There are a set of separate yards between the cell buildings, where the prisoners have an hour for exercise each day.

The Catholic Church service is held in the center; the cell doors are locked open about three inches, which enables the prisoners to hear and see. There is but one door to the cell, which is a close plank door, and is kept closed at all other times. The corridors are lighted from skylights, but they are not sufficient in size or number. Any work done is in the cells, such as making buttons from the ivory nut, or cards to wind silk on, some shoes. The work does not count for much. The sentence is for labor, and an effort is earnestly made to comply with it. I was pleased to have seen the Madras Prison, as it has frequently been referred to as one of the great prisons of Europe. I was five hours in this prison, and saw it all, from the cellar to the roof. A military guard is stationed in the yard, at each corner of the wall. I went from the Madras Prison with the feeling of having seen much but learned nothing. I next went to the

DE LA SANTE PRISON,

where I was received by the Director, A. Laguesse, who was very courteous and desirous I should see all that was of interest. I found him quite familiar with the work he is engaged in, and understands the Philadelphia system, as he terms it, in contradistinction to the Auburn system.

In his office there are ground plans of both the Auburn and Eastern Penitentiaries. This prison was built on the plan of the Eastern Penitentiary, the blocks radiating from a center, with cells on each side of the corridor. One-half of this prison is used for cellular treatment positively; in the other half the prisoners go out to work in shops in congregation, same as in our American prisons generally.   There were about eight hundred inmates, one-half of whom were under individual treatment.   Captain Laguesse understands what he is doing.   All first convictions are in the cellular side of the prison, and are treated individually, unless some physical or mental infirmity would indicate that the other would be best for such persons; some of the récidivistes are also treated separately.   The rule is not positive for either class.   The Director's judgment determines which is the proper treatment for all prisoners.   Captain Laguesse is entirely capable of determining which is the proper treatment in any case.   He has been twenty-eight years in this service, not all the time in this prison.   The service there is continuous and controlled by the Department of the Interior; officers may be removed from one prison to another, but still remain in the prison service.   Captain Laguesse, of the 114th Territorial Infantry, is the station he holds in the regular government service.

Religious service is held every Sunday.

There is a chapel where the Protestant service is held for those of that faith confined in the prison.

The prisoners go into this separate chapel and occupy separate seats, not seeing each other; but all see the minister and he sees all of them.

In the center there is an elevated structure about twelve feet high and ten feet in diameter, on top of which there is an altar, where mass is said by the priest.   The prisoners can all hear and most of them can see the priest from their cells.   The lower part of this structure is used as an office for the chief warder.   Supervision of the entire interior of the prison is had from this point.   There are no iron doors to the cells; one wooden door, which is locked open about five inches during religious service.   The cells are about same dimension as the cells in the Madras Prison, lighted and ventilated by the same method.   Cell ornaments are not permitted.   An iron bedstead; when in use it is about six inches from the floor; it is turned up on its side, close to the wall, during the day.   The blankets and sheets are folded neatly on top of it.   A table and stool fastened to the wall by a chain, wash-basins, and shelf are all the furniture.   There is a gas jet in each cell, fixed in a space in the wall about eight inches square.   On the cell side of this opening there is a strong glass not easily broken.   The light is at no time under the control of the prisoner.   This arrangement gives the officers good opportunity for supervision. The cell walls are of brick, plastered with cement, and painted in two colors. The walls, about four feet high, are painted brown, above that white. The corridors are painted in like manner. The same system of water-closet sewerage as at the Madras Prison, which method is condemned by both directors. Prisoners' friends are permitted to visit weekly, which the Director says is too frequent, and does more harm than good. The industries are such as can be had, making dolls and stamping paper for flowers, tailoring, and shoe-making. There are fifty officers, besides the military guard placed on duty in the yard and outside at the front entrance. There has never been a successful escape; several attempts have been made.

This prison has been in use twenty-seven years, and is now in as good order as any prison can be. Washing the clothes is done outside, in the Paris laundries. The bread is good, made principally of rye flour; meat twice a week. Prisoners are permitted to purchase extra food from the prison kitchen when they have the means of paying for it.

Any one who knows anything about prisons can see that the Director understands all the details of the management of this prison.

Penitentiaire De Fouilleuse.

I next went out to Fouilleuse près Rueil, about twelve miles, where there is an institution for the correction of girls under sixteen years of age. There were then three hundred inmates; some are placed there by their parents, others by the courts for misdemeanors. They are divided into separate associations. They are cared for properly, and are taught to work from the first day they enter the institution. The little ones were preparing parts of shirts used with other more important parts necessary to make up a shirt. Other older girls were engaged in making cravats, fancy and plain. This is intelligent work, the knowledge of which will be useful to the girls after leaving the institution. The important feature of any work done in institutions is the usefulness of the articles when made. This place is two miles from the railroad station. The surrounding country is laid out in farms for raising vegetables for the Paris market.

Madame Henri Hubert, the Directress, received me very cordially. She went with me to every part of her domain, in which she takes special pride; she is entirely capable of doing the work she has in hand. There is no force used here. No wall, no bars, nothing that would give the place any appearance of forcible detention. Madame Hubert says none go away; they could if they wanted to. They are permitted to go out on Sundays; they always return on time. There is no drill, no machine training to show visitors when they come how near alike all the inmates are. These children look up as if they were at home; no fear of punishment nor of threatened punishment.

This is the best method of treating children I have seen anywhere. There are about twenty acres of ground belonging to the institution under cultivation. Madame Hubert is happily adapted for the work she is engaged in.

PETITE ROQUETTE.

Correction for boys. The structure was erected on the plan of the Millbank Prison in London, and was originally used for a separate prison, but is now used as a house of correction. There were three hundred and fifty boys under eighteen years of age in the institution. Some are in separate cells, some work together in shops on light work, such as can be obtained and they can be taught.

Some of the boys are convicted of crime, but most of them are incorrigible and placed there by parents. The treatment is mild, and the Director seems to know what he is doing. When the parents desire they can take their boy out, and put him back if they cannot manage him.

The structure is an old one, and not in good condition. It was built in 1836, more than half a century ago. The buildings have been neglected, without any effort to make any repairs to parts decayed or worn out.

Directly opposite, on the other side of the street, fronts another prison, the Roquette, where convicts are awaiting after conviction to be distributed to the several prisons as their case and condition may require. Executions take place here by guillotine, which is done in public in front of the prison gate. I did not go into the Roquette Prison. I had no interest in learning anything about executions or the methods necessary for performing any of the duties required of a public executioner. I went to the

CONCIERGERIE,

the old prison at the palace of justice known as the Conciergerie. This prison is used for persons when first apprehended or waiting trial. The Director, Captain Gaude, received me very kindly, stating that the Minister of the Interior had sent notice that I would visit that prison. This is an old structure of the Gothic style of architecture of the finest work. It is really grand. It was built six hundred years ago. Was formerly used as a residence of kings of France. It is in good condition now, clean in every part, evidently well managed and properly directed. The cells are large, well lighted, and in good order. The floors are of wood, walls painted, window in rear of cell. The doors are wood, no inside iron doors; separate exercising yards. The same system of drainage from the cells as at the De la Sante and the Madras prisons. The refuse is received in an iron receptacle placed in the cellar, water running through continuously. These receiving vessels are cleaned out once a week. Director Gaude told me that the department officials were considering the subject of cell drainage, with a view of improving the present method. Many historic incidents are connected with this prison. It was here that the massacre of St. Bartholomew took place, and where the queen, Marie Antoinette, was confined awaiting execution. The room occupied by her is in the same condition as when she went from it to the guillotine. Here the Girondists were confined. The room in which they took their last breakfast remains in the same condition as when they went from it to execution. Madame Roland was confined here, and went out with the other Girondists, of which party she was a leader. The execution of this woman was one of the sad events of the French Revolution. There are few places in the world where more distressing events have occurred than in this "Conciergerie" Prison.

On August 27th left Paris for Brussels at 8.15 A.M.; arrived there at 3 P.M. I went next morning to see about getting into the Belgian prisons. I was directed to the palace of justice. I waited on the Minister of Justice, who very kindly gave me an official order to visit all the prisons of Belgium. All prisons in Belgium are under the direction of the Minister of Justice. I first went to the new

PRISON ST. GILLES,

recently completed and directed by J. Stevens, who at once recognized me by name, having had the reports of the Eastern State Penitentiary continuously. He has been in the service forty years and is conversant with all the details of the subject. He has been frequently in communication with our Mr. Vaux on the subject of treatment of criminals and crime. Mr. Stevens is an intelligent man, speaks and writes well on the subject. After some conversation with him we were shown through the prison in all its parts. The separate cellular system is carried out properly. There are six hundred cells in all and about five hundred prisoners confined. They work in the cells. Everything is new and bright. Mr. Stevens superintended the erection of the prison. He introduced any improvements he deemed advantageous to the system. The sewer-pipe and water-closet in the cell he abandoned, and substituted the bucket plan, which I think is a mistake.

The buckets are taken out of the cells every morning and others put in at the same time. It requires two sets. At the end of each gallery is a sewer. The buckets are taken there and emptied.

There are three chapels on the separate stall plan, Catholic, Protestant, and Hebrew.

There are six blocks three tiers high, with a glass roof over the corridor. There is abundance of light in this prison. The walls of the cells and corridors are painted. The floors are of tile. Complaints of prisoners are heard by the Director every morning in open court. The prisoner is brought into a room for the purpose. He makes his charge or states his grievance in presence of the overseer or officer having charge of him. The officer is at liberty to question and reply to the charge made. The Director decides the case. I next went to

LOUVAIN,

which is an hour and a half from Brussels through a splendid garden country. I was at once admitted into the prison. The Director received me kindly; he was desirous of my seeing all of the prison and everything connected with it. He gave me in charge of an officer who has been forty years in the prison service, who was familiar with all the details. This is the Philadelphia prison, and is so designated. The plans are marked in that way. The blocks are three tiers high, with cells on either side of the corridor about the same dimensions as in the other prison; six hundred cells and nearly that many prisoners. The system is carried out as it was intended. All work done in the cells. Exercising yards between the blocks. There are many life-sentenced prisoners in consequence of there being no death penalty in Belgium.

Separate exercising yards between the blocks. Separation is carried out as it was intended. The work is done in the cells—shoemaking, tailoring, and matmaking. The system of drainage by soil pipes is as it was when the prison was erected. The water supply is in tanks placed under the roof; the water pumped up by hand. There are several separate pumps in cells. The prisoners occupying these cells work these pumps.

The relatives visit the prisoners once in three months as a rule, oftener than that by special order. All visitors are under strict supervision. There are stalls just large enough for a person to stand in. These stalls face each other with a wire netting in front of each, and a two-foot space between the stalls where an officer is placed for the purpose of supervision. It may not be an agreeable method for visiting friends, but it insures surveillance if the officer is observant. After all, the doing of everything depends on how it is done. There is evident care and attention in the management and direction and supervision of the Louvain Prison. Those in charge are earnest in their endeavor to promote the best interests of the work conscientiously and with intelligent judgment, and seem assured that their method of treatment for criminals is productive of the best results for the protection of society and benefit of the prisoners when released.

The prisons of four countries that I visited are distinct in all respects. The physical make-up of the people of these countries is different. Habits, dispositions, manners, and language mark each country as peculiarly distinctive.

While every provision is made for the care and detention of the prison inmates, there is little or no consideration given to the individual peculiarities of the criminal, or no thought as I saw manifested how best they can be directed away from the causes that placed them in their present situation in life.

In each of these countries the laws, and penalties for their violation, are different. In Ireland and England the inmates of the convict prisons in physical appearance are much the same. They are mostly below thirty-five years of age, many of which are first convictions, and not of the crime-class. These facts do not seem to be considered, or any means employed to rescue individuals from the accumulating crime-class. The principle adopted is to reform all.

The governments, climate, laws, penalties, crime, environments, and people of these countries are different and distinctive, as are the individuals which make up the populations of these several countries in which the prisons I visited are located.

I did not examine anything of the system of moral influences in these prisons. What I saw made these impressions, but it would be unjust to all to express opinions on what I did not see fully. I seem to think that the governments of those countries cannot run these institutions as we in this country think they ought to be carried on. In our prisons the system is dependent for its results on the officials of the prisons. The best system will be ruined by a bad administration, and even a bad system will turn out well if well carried out. The Warden is the real, practical, responsible director of a prison.

Having seen all of the Louvain Prison I returned to Paris, leaving Brussels at 1.15 P.M., arrived in Paris at 6.30, where I remained until the sailing of the steamship "Bretagne," which left Havre on the 21st of September. In eight days from that time I arrived in Philadelphia, United States of America. The first thing to do upon arrival was to go to the prison located there. This prison is known as the

EASTERN STATE PENITENTIARY

for the Eastern District of Pennsylvania. It is situated in the city of Philadelphia, on the north side of Fairmount Avenue, near the Schuylkill River and Fairmount Park.

This penitentiary occupies ten acres of ground inclosed by a wall thirty-two feet high. The front gate and only entrance opens

Front View of Exterior.

on Fairmount Avenue. The administration building on the front is of gray granite, purely Gothic in architecture. The front entrance is through a fine Gothic arch thirty feet in height, sixteen feet in width to an inside gate, sixty feet between the two gates. Only one of these gates is open at the same time; when a vehicle passes in from the street the outer gate is closed before the inside gate is opened.

In the same way wagons, etc., are passed out. The gate-keepers are always present, one at the front and one at the inner gate. The eastern section of the front building is used for the warden's residence and the inspectors have their room on that side. The western section is for the resident physician and matron.

The center building from which the cell structures radiate is in the center of the ten-acre plot of ground. This center building is forty feet in diameter, each corridor opens into it. There are ten corridors; six of them are one story, the other four are two stories. Seven blocks were originally intended to complete the cell structures. The green lawn that extended from the inside gate to the center building has been utilized for the erection of one hundred cells. These cells or rooms would be the proper term for them, are eight by eighteen feet, eleven feet high, lighted by two skylights in the roof, an inner iron door with an outer door of wood which slides in grooves. These rooms open upon a corridor ten feet wide, sixteen feet high, lighted from the roof by a sufficient number of skylights to insure abundant light on the darkest days. The doors of these rooms are locked open all the time, night and day. These rooms are supplied with as much water as the inmates desire to use. There is an incandescent electric light in each room. The prisoner has the use of the light until nine o'clock. The furniture consists of bed-stand of wood, made as simple and inexpensive as possible, the frequent renewal of which conduces to the sanitary condition of the rooms. Each room contains mess pan, plate, spoon, knife and fork, dust-brush, hand-scrubs, hair-comb, shaving-brush, two towels and soap. Razors are supplied once a week for any one who desire to use them. A loose tick filled with straw for bed, three sheets, two pillow-slips, two or more blankets, as required. Each bed has a quilted cover. Every prisoner has an entire new bed outfit on his admission. The bedding is renewed frequently. These corridors, being out of the line of the original radiating plan, are under supervision from the center building by two large mirrors, set in a position that reflects all of these corridors to the center officer. There is always an officer on duty in the center. The entire structure, containing seven hundred and thirty-one rooms, is under observation from that point.

The other cell structures were built previous to 1829 when the penitentiary was first opened for the admission of prisoners. Exercising yards are connected with the cells on the ground floor. These yards are eight by eighteen, with walls eleven feet high. The cells open into these yards through an iron latticed door on the inside of the cell wall. A wooden outer door secures the opening. The wooden door is open continuously. The door opening into the corridor being also open continuously makes a strong current of air passing through the rooms all the time. There is a six-inch flue leading from each cell to the top of the roof. There is no doubt about the ventilation being sufficient. Water and electric light in every cell. The grounds are also supplied with abundant light from thirty arc lights of two thousand candle-power covering every part of the inclosure. The soil pipes leading from the water-closets are eight inches in diameter and are kept full of water. They are flushed out twice each day. They empty into a trapped inlet that exhausts into a sewer. Sewer gas cannot pass through the soil pipes, as they are full of water. Forty thousand gallons of water are required for the use of the penitentiary daily. A constant reserve of three hundred thousand gallons of water is kept on hand at all times in a reservoir of that capacity. There is a ten-horse engine and a pump of ten thousand gallons capacity per hour always ready for use. This engine also drives a flour mill which makes all the flour used in the penitentiary. The grain is purchased from the near-by farmers, which is always new and good.

There is a resident physician in attendance at all hours. The sick are attended in their room as they would be at their home. Convalescents are exercised in the spaces between the cell structures, there being ample room for the purpose. The weak-lunged are also exercised in this way. This is not play or an excuse to evade other duties. They must keep up a regular brisk walk for thirty minutes, which is as much as one in their condition can do at one time. An efficient officer attends to this work exclusively.

All supplies for this penitentiary are purchased in the open market for cash, under direction of the board of inspectors, who are appointed by the Governor of the State.

The prisoners are employed at various branches of industry—men's shoemaking, women's shoemaking, in separate departments, knitting hosiery, matmaking, cigarmaking, chairmaking, weaving, brushmaking.

The government consists of five inspectors appointed by the Governor of the State for the term of two years each. They elect the warden, doctor, clerk, and appoint a moral instructor. The warden is the executive officer, appoints all subordinate officers, and is held responsible by the board for the well-being of the penitentiary. There are forty-five officers of all grades. They are trained and educated for this service. Their tenure of office is continuous, removals are only for cause. The lowest grade is night watchman, of whom there are six. All persons employed enter the service as night watchmen, from which grade promotions are made to other departments as vacancies occur. Remuneration increases with promotion and length of time in the service.

There are no dark cells or any mechanical appliances for punishment; none are needed under the methods of treatment pursued in this penitentiary.

At some future time I may make more extended explanations of my observations of the Eastern State Penitentiary, as it is open for investigation by any person interested in the subject of prison structure and system of treatment of the inmates.

The direction and management of the Eastern State Penitentiary is not as most other prisons, a machine, that when a part gives out deranges the whole. Any part may become deranged or get out of order without effecting any other part. Any occurrence that may take place is confined to the immediate locality in which it occurred. Force is not required to direct or control a single individual. In this method of treatment not so much depends on the ability or experience of the director as with any other method of prison management. The individual treatment system will succeed under the direction of any management that will adhere to its principles.

I thank you, gentlemen, for your patient attention to my defense of the charge preferred against me by the President of the Wardens' Association. If you are not fully convinced of my inability to attend the Cincinnati meeting, I beg of you to suspend judgment until some further evidence can be produced that a "dunce who has been to Rome does not excel a dunce that stayed at home."